THE
PHYSICIAN'S
ROADMAP
TO PERSONAL & FINANCIAL FREEDOM

How to Unlock
Opportunities
and Create Options

THE
PHYSICIAN'S
ROADMAP
TO PERSONAL &
FINANCIAL FREEDOM

AMIT SAHASRABUDHE, MD, MS

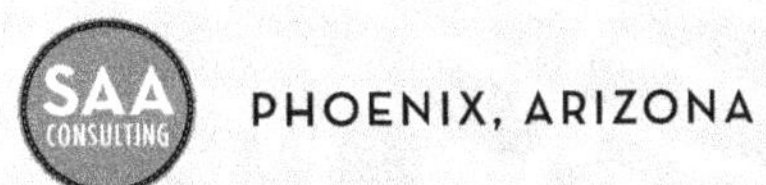

PHOENIX, ARIZONA

*To all the aspiring and practicing physicians
who want the most from their medical career.*

Contents

Foreword

BEING A PHYSICIAN is a great honor and opportunity. . .
and a great deal of hard work. Lifelong learning, the opportunity to serve, and a recession-proof income confer privilege.
Yet competition for coveted positions, rigorous training, and
the challenges of patient care create stress. Although physicians are well compensated, this compensation is mitigated
by a substantial delay in an ability to begin saving (due to the
years required for medical and post-graduate training), the
high overhead required for medical practice (impactful even
for employed physicians), ever-decreasing reimbursement,
and ever-increasing administrative burdens, and obstacles,
requiring navigation in order to be paid.

Cue the small violins. We are passionate about what we do.
While burnout may come and go, in the end, we find balance.
We remain respected in our communities and fulfilled by
our accomplishments. Still, it would be nice if it were "just
a little easier."

In this book, Amit Sahasrabudhe attempts to make things
a little easier for doctors by guiding us with practical and tested tips, pearls, and "optionality" to help physicians achieve
financial security and independence in our challenging

healthcare economic environment. While some, including me, may lean toward delicacy when discussing financial matters, Amit, to his credit, pulls no punches. To the benefit of readers, he tells it like it is and lifts the proverbial veil, providing a foundation for a physician-specific education in personal finance.

Amit shares his mistakes, his successes, and what he has learned. Among his most valuable suggestions (as I have learned through my own missteps) is that physicians need to collaborate with consultants.

In addition to reading and attempting to understand every word of any contract before signing it, we must never fail to consult our lawyer, accountant, and financial planner on any decision or matter of consequence. If we find ourselves wondering, "*Should I run this by my lawyer, CPA, or financial planner?*". . . well, if we have to ask, we already know the answer. The answer is unquestionably "Yes."

This book is a primer. Every situation is different, and our world continues to evolve. We must not rely exclusively on any single piece of advice, even one introduced after a foreword I have written. Rather, reading and revisiting this valuable publication is a first step, prompting us to pursue our own path, perform our further due diligence, and conscientiously consult our personal team of legal and financial advisors.

My path in medicine has been varied; quite different from Amit's; entirely different from anything I could have imagined when I started; and eminently rewarding. Yet it certainly would have "been just a little bit easier" had I had access to this book years ago. By presenting a physician-specific, personal finance education that "they didn't teach you in medical school," Amit shares his roadmap to physician financial freedom. This should help diminish stress and reduce burnout, to the ultimate benefit of our patients. By improving our own financial health, we can better focus on the health of our patients, with an ultimate goal of best being of service.

—**James Lubowitz, MD**

Introduction

IT'S TWO DAYS BEFORE MATCH DAY, March 2001. In the era before email, I was anxious to get the envelope that told me where I was headed for residency.

Instead, I faced an event that no fourth-year med student wants to experience. I was sitting in an elective class with a bunch of classmates.

And my phone rang.

Everybody looked around at me, wide-eyed. Surely, I was one of the people who would match.

On the other end of the line, I heard my dean's voice. "Amit, hey, it's Dr. Aach, and I regret to tell you that you didn't match. When you have a chance, come meet with me and we can talk about what we can do from here."

Match Day is supposed to be the pinnacle of happiness and relief for a med student, even more than graduation day: You finally have the initial roadmap for where you're going and what you'll be doing for the next few years of your life.

Instead, now I was stuck in "the scramble": scrambling to find a residency spot somewhere—anywhere!—in any area of medicine that I might want to consider. It took an already stressful time and exponentially blew it out of the water. I was miserable. While the rest of my classmates were celebrating on Match Day, I skipped out. What was the point? I couldn't believe this was happening.

For a very brief period of time, I was committed to doing a preliminary general surgery internship at a hospital in Pittsburgh, thinking, "Well, I guess I could try reapplying next year to orthopedics, or maybe I'll just do heart surgery, which is what I was going to do when I first started med school. I don't know, maybe I should just do something else with my life."

I was not in a good place. But eventually things got better—much better.

I did end up practicing orthopedics. I built, grew, and maintained a successful private practice from both a clinical care perspective and as a financially successful business. I became, and continue to be, a sought-after physician in the expert witness world in multiple states. As a team physician, I started out working with high schools in Scottsdale, Arizona; eventually this led to being on the sidelines with the NFL's Arizona Cardinals, behind the bench with the NHL's then-Phoenix Coyotes, and in the dugout with the Chicago Cubs, Oakland A's, Colorado Rockies, and San Francisco Giants in Major League Baseball. In fact, the Cubs flew me to Wrigley Field for the home games during the 2016 World Series, and somehow they managed to fit my ridiculously long last name on a championship ring with 108 diamonds on it—one for every year since their last title.

When I was playing baseball as a kid, I never
imagined that I'd have one of these.

My original intention was to retire at 50, assuming I didn't want to continue practicing. But I managed to do it at 48, through a strategy that I've shared in the following 200 or so pages. I gave myself optionality—and you can too.

Navigating the Challenges of a Medical Career

If you picked up this book, whether on your own or because someone recommended it to you—regardless of being a med student, resident or fellow, or a practicing physician looking for a change—I'm going to take a guess why:

- You're concerned about medical pay being static or going down relative to inflation and the cost of living.

- You're annoyed, because medicine hasn't turned out to be what you thought it was going to be or you're not enjoying practicing as much as you believed you would.

- You're not getting paid as much as you assumed you would, or could or should, based on your education, training, and how much time you spend working.

- You're looking for options to help pay off your student loans faster.

- You're not satisfied with just practicing medicine—and you know there are other opportunities out there that you can leverage with your medical degree.

We have these notions of what doing something will be like, whether that's practicing medicine or law, running a small business, or serving as the mayor of your hometown. Until you're actually doing it, you can't possibly know what it's like, regardless of industry or career. Sure, friends, family, and neighbors might tell you their own personal experience, or maybe your mom or dad was a physician. But no matter how many common threads there might be, you will have your own unique experience, and you won't fully understand it till you're in the thick of it. **We *don't know what we don't know*.** That comes with highs and lows, and both of them need to be managed. You may get into situations where you're feeling invincible and others where you're miserable. Take a moment. Pause. Assess.

It's hard enough to become a physician. Then it can feel like you're being held hostage once you get there, because you spent so much blood, sweat, tears, time, and money to achieve it, and change seems daunting. If that's how you're feeling, you're not alone:

- According to a survey conducted by the Medical Group Management Association (MGMA) and recruiting firm Jackson Physician Search, **the mean duration at an initial job** for physicians who completed their residency or fellowship in the previous six years **was less than two years.**[1]

- A Physicians Foundation survey in 2023 found that **six in 10 physicians often have feelings of burnout**, compared to four in 10 in 2018. Like their physician colleagues, **six in 10 residents often have feelings of burnout**, while that number jumps to **seven in 10 for medical students.**[2]

- The AMA's 2024 Organizational Biopsy found that **31.9% of doctors** said they had "**a moderate interest in leaving their current jobs within the next two years**, or that they would like to or definitely would leave in that time period."[3]

- According to a longitudinal study by the Annals of Internal Medicine, "unadjusted rates of **clinical practice attrition increased significantly from 3.5% in 2013 to 4.9% in 2019.**" Attrition increased for everyone:

---

1   "New Physicians Leave First Jobs Within 2 Years: MGMA Study," April 16, 2025, https://www.physiciansweekly.com/post/why-many-physicians-do-not-stay-at-their-first-jobs-for-the-long-term

2   "The Physicians Foundation's 2023 Survey of America's Current and Future Physicians," https://physiciansfoundation.org/research/amplifying-physician-resident-and-student-voices-to-drive-wellbeing-and-care-delivery-solutions

3   "Physicians in these 10 specialties are less likely to quit," June 24, 2025, https://www.ama-assn.org/practice-management/physician-health/physicians-these-10-specialties-are-less-likely-quit

male and female, across specialties and geographic regions.[4]

Let me be crystal clear: I'm not trying to be a downer or to make you second-guess your chosen career. Quite the opposite. The goal is to expose you to options that leverage the most marketable degree around and keep you engaged in medicine. Even if your organization doesn't value you properly, or if you are experiencing challenges in private practice, you need to take action on your own.

So, how do you get there? Among the topics we'll cover:

- What details you need to know about potential employers or partners—before you sign on the dotted line.

- How to develop a profitable practice model that isn't 100% reliant on patient care—and provides better work-life balance.

- Why state medical licenses are like a secret key that unlocks multiple doors—and why to get them as early in your career as possible.

- How a better understanding of contracts and insurance codes might add tens or hundreds of thousands of dollars to your revenues every single year—without extra work.

- What the best alternatives are to seeing patients that still leverage your medical expertise—such as expert witness work, consulting, and more.

---

4   "Trends in and Predictors of Physician Attrition From Clinical Practice Across Specialties: A Nationwide, Longitudinal Analysis," October 7, 2025, https://www.acpjournals.org/doi/10.7326/ANNALS-25-00564

- Why physicians and real estate can make an excellent match—and how you can get started.

- What steps you need to take to protect your financial well-being—including insights from experts who work with physicians and their money.

- How to position yourself for the future, whether you intend to retire early or practice forever.

Don't Walk Away—Create Your Own Roadmap

Looking back on 25-plus years of experience and thousands of patients, there are a lot of things I wish I'd known when I started out—most notably, the aspects of the real world that they don't teach in undergrad, med school, residency, or fellowship. You either learn it because you have interest and aptitude, you learn it the hard way by screwing up, or you never learn and end up feeling like you're stuck in a rut.

I've been where you are, and my failures weren't limited to that ill-fated Match Day during which I went matchless. The first time I took the orthopedics oral board exam, for example, I botched it. Although I passed the written component, I was woefully unprepared for the oral exam. For what seemed like an eternity, I was grilled by six orthopedic surgeons about the intricacies of 10 surgical cases I'd done over the previous six months, and their nonstop tangents broke my train of thought and took me down. I prepared differently—more like getting ready for grand rounds—and passed it the next time. Nonetheless, it was a wake-up call.

An even harsher reality check had occurred during my

second year of residency, at University of Pittsburgh Medical Center (UPMC). Spine call was shared by Orthopedics & Neurosurgery; we took the odd months, they took the even months. One night I was called to the ER to consult on a patient who had a spine concern, and I could instinctively tell they just. . . didn't like me. Sure enough, they later claimed that I hadn't done a proper physical exam. Making matters worse, it escalated from the ER attending to the Orthopedic Surgery chairman, and both of them took the patient's side.

First, I don't match, then I'm stressed out by the number of hours (there was no 80-hour work week max for residents back then) and intensity of ER call, only to have my department abandon me. "You know what?" I thought to myself. "I don't need this crap. Maybe I'm not cut out for this. I don't know what I'm going to do, but it's going to be something else."

With visions of quitting still rattling around in my head, I ended up on a rotation in orthopedic trauma. I'd known the trauma attending since med school and he'd been my advocate when I applied for residency to Pitt, so we'd gotten to know each other. He could tell I wasn't in a good space, so he sat down with me and asked, "Is everything okay?" I told him the basics of my story. He nodded and said, "Look, I agree that that's BS, but this type of crap is going to happen, and you have to deal with it one way or another. Even if you're not doing this anymore, there will be some different crap over there. Residency sucks right now, but it will get better. I encourage you to just stay the course."

It was good advice, and I did stick with it. I almost walked away, but here I am. Then again, in my own way, I did walk down a different path from most of my peers while remaining in medicine. That route, as winding as it was, delivered meaning beyond just treating patients.

It's Time to Remove Your Blinders

Up to this point in your career, you've probably known for a long time that you wanted to be a physician. In high school and college, your took classes geared towards the next step in the process. If you were strategic, you knew that the MCAT was going to require biology or organic chemistry, and maybe you took physiology because it would be helpful in med school, even though you'd need to do a deeper dive once you got there.

In a way, though, that unrelenting focus on studying hard, getting good grades, and achieving the next level can come with a side effect. The blinders that helped you tune out the rest of the world and avoid distractions can become a hindrance once you're a practicing physician. All around you are opportunities, but you need to see them, recognize them, and be open to them.

During your medical training, you learned a process that can be applied to your career, no matter where you are in it. You don't go into every complex circumstance or diagnosis assuming that you know exactly what's going on. You need to figure out what the systems are, and how they are involved.

In a way, your career is a lifelong lesson in anatomy, with systems that can be examined and diagnosed separately—but they also interact with each other in ways that are not always apparent at first glance. I'll assume you have medical knowledge and talent. But you need to take the blinders off, or at least poke some holes in them. You've been using your powers of observation and analysis all along to get where you are. Why would you stop that process when you become a physician, and only focus on how things affect you in the current moment? What about tomorrow and 10 or 20 years from now, and the options you might need?

Too many physicians fail to realize how powerful it is to have a medical degree, or neglect to tap into it. Those two letters after your name have an outsized impact, wherever you are in the world and no matter who you're talking to. Anyone from a construction worker to a stockbroker to an architect understands that medical training is long and grueling, even if they don't know exactly what's involved. You're given street cred right from the jump, and can parlay that far beyond medicine.

The Power of Dictating Your Own Path

I owe a great deal to my career in medicine; it eventually provided opportunities that I couldn't imagine when I'd been up for 24 hours at 3 a.m., sewing somebody back together in the ER. I had the good fortune of learning lessons from some brilliant teachers, colleagues, and business partners throughout my career. (And let's not forget to thank a few folks who served as examples of what not to do or how to act.) So, I look at this book as a way of paying it forward, addressing what I believe are some critical shortcomings in our medical education system, and sharing strategies that you can use to succeed beyond your expectations. This book isn't intended to educate you on all the nitty-gritty details of doing certain things. It's designed to introduce some of your possible options, and to get you thinking "What else I can do?"

That said, success is personal. It's not necessarily that you're making $1 million a year, or that you have a given title, or that you've got your name on a new surgical technique or slapped on the side of a med school building. Success is whatever you want to make of it. At the end of the day, no matter what you do, you need to hustle. **No one likes a lazy person.**

As noted above, I've made my share of mistakes, and you're going to make some of your own. I've worked in jobs that I didn't love (and some that I hated), and you probably will too.

But trust me on this: By creating optionality in your medical career, you'll dramatically increase your odds of being successful, however you want to define it.

As you commence into the rest of this book, I want you to have a concept in the back of your mind. I'll address it more in the final chapter, but I believe it will help you create a framework in your brain to absorb everything I'm describing—whether you decide to do it or not.

The concept is this: It's human nature to think that the purpose or meaning in your life needs to be the same till the day you die. When you were a little kid and someone asked you who you were, you'd respond with your name. Years later, your identity becomes your life stage, so you'd say, "I'm in med school."

Now, depending on where you are in your career, you'd say what kind of doctor you are. It's a sneaky change, in which your identity becomes rooted in what your work is. The risk, in my opinion, is how that can create resistance in making course alterations to your purpose and meaning in life. It's another set of blinders, if you're not aware of it.

Some doctors love helping people, some love to operate, some love the challenge of curing obscure diseases, and still others are sparked by a pure curiosity about human anatomy and physiology. (And let's not pretend that money isn't a motivation too.) Maybe that passion extends through your entire career, and you're still learning every day. Maybe you enjoy it so much that you keep practicing till death do you part, or that in retirement you travel the world treating people through a charitable organization.

Realistically, however, there's a point of diminishing returns with your skill set and desire. I've known people who've gone on to medical-related second careers, only to boomerang back to practicing medicine. Others stayed with medicine the whole time, but took off to a different city. Some hung it up, and then either were bored, frustrated, or not making enough money, and they decided to go back. And still others started or worked in businesses that had nothing to do with medicine.

I've written this book to equip you to make those decisions yourself, not to have your roadmap dictated for you. It's the ultimate freedom.

—Amit Sahasrabudhe, MD, MS
February 2026

YOU DON'T NEED
TO GO IT ALONE

For most of us, when we have anything but the simplest issue with our car, it's time to head to the mechanic. Think about it in medical terms: If you're an otolaryngologist and someone asks you a question about their heart, you might be able to educate them on the basics you remember from medical school. But if it's even slightly complicated or concerning, you're sending them to a cardiologist.

We refer patients all the time when a patient's ailment is outside our specialty or subspecialty... so why is it that so many of us feel unreasonably confident about real-world situations outside our expertise? The heart of this book is about exposing you to concepts and options that you may encounter or want to consider—but all of them will go more smoothly if you enlist the help of an expert or someone with experience, whether a trusted medical colleague, CPA, financial advisor, business consultant, or lawyer in a particular field. You may have spent hundreds of thousands on your medical degree. Once you're out in the real world making money, I encourage you to invest in professional guidance to keep yourself out of hot water and avoid red tape. I'll continue to remind you of that throughout this book—including two bonus chapters that were written by professionals (a financial advisor and a CPA) who have extensive experience working with physicians.

CHAPTER 1

Looking for Your First Job

Creating Options as You Enter

the Working World

WHETHER YOUR MEDICAL DIPLOMA doesn't even have dust on it, or you're unhappy with the job you're in and want to hunt for something different, you likely have more questions than answers. Where do I even begin? Where do I look? Do I post on LinkedIn? Text my residency director? Call the chairman? Send an email to a colleague I knew along the way? The answer to all of those is Yes.

Before you even start the job hunt, the bigger question to ask yourself is: What kind of medicine do I want to practice? By that, I don't mean whether you want to be a pediatrician, oncologist, or surgeon. What I mean is: What are the nuances of what I'm going to do if I join a given practice? That framework will help guide where you look and what you look for, long before you need to make a decision. And, of course, the broader your scope, the more optionality you bring to your search—and your eventual roadmap.

Key Resources When You're Hunting for a Job

RECRUITERS

Most people will be surprised that during the end of residency or in fellowship, postcards and flyers will show up at your desk, in your mail at home, or in email. Like it or not, there are huge databases out there that recruiters have access to, and their job is to connect a graduating resident/fellow with a practice, hospital, or large group. When an entity has an opening and a recruiter makes a fit, that entity is paying the recruiter. Note that this doesn't need to be a passive, wait-and-see situation—you can reach out to recruiters on your own by networking on sites such as LinkedIn, and letting them be your eyes and ears.

The first reason recruiters are a good starting place is that their network gives them access to any and all areas that are advertising for openings. Now, that doesn't mean it's always the best job, but the second reason to start there is that working with a recruiter is a way to learn what to look for, and questions to ask. And it's great because it doesn't cost you anything other than your time. They will bring up things that you may not have thought of. You can bring up things the recruiter may not know an answer to, but can ask a potential employer and potentially come up with something that's negotiable. Above all, you will learn from the ebb and flow of the exchange. If you get a couple of interviews out of it, even if you know going into it that it's probably not a job that you want, there's no substitute for practice interviews to gain further skill and experience. You'll learn what employers and medical practices are looking for, what phrasing works, and you can practice your questioning skills in a situation that isn't necessarily high stakes.

My first interview was through a recruiter. The hospital flew me out to a wine region, had one of the orthopedic surgeons pick me in his BMW M5, and drive me through back roads, whizzing around. It was fun and it felt like they really wanted me—they even put me up at a gorgeous B&B at a vineyard. It's not uncommon for remotely located medical practices to roll out the red carpet for you in order to attract you to practice where there's a need but fewer physicians choose to live. I learned a lot from the experience, including what I didn't want.

SPECIALTY JOURNALS

No matter what specialty you are in, there are journals that publish literature and research in the field. Even in an era where it seems like everything is virtual, this is a time where a print publication can be a benefit in addition to whatever online listings are available. Look for the jobs section and you'll find job ads by city, town, state, and nuances of the job. Even if the description isn't perfect—maybe you don't want to take ER call—it might be worth contacting them.

CONFERENCES

While your main goal for attending a particular conference is probably the topic and maybe some continuing medical education credits, it can be a valuable way to do some job hunting even when you are a resident or fellow. I can attest to this, because I got my first job through a conference. I was debating going to a conference on cartilage restoration in Southern California or a business-focused conference in

Phoenix. When I asked my fellowship director, he suggested that I'd get more out of the business session.

On day one, I combed through the big syllabus binder that listed all of the attendees and where they lived and worked. I paid special attention to the names in Phoenix, since it was one of the places I was considering moving to. At the final session, I casually said hi to the woman on my right—and I did a double-take, as I recognized her name as someone from the Phoenix metro area. During a pause in the lecture, we struck up a conversation, and it turned out she was the business administrator of a group that was looking to fill a position that they hadn't and weren't planning on advertising. Better yet, one of the two partners was there and she introduced me to him.

There was a sticky wicket, however: I was supposed to fly out that night to go skiing with my wife in Taos, New Mexico. I quickly thought through the pros and cons, then decided to stay another night in Phoenix, and meet with them the next day. I could have said, "I'm heading out of town, can I get back to you?" Maybe it would have worked out anyway, but it seemed like one of those times to seize the opportunity. They hired me, and that first job was a steppingstone to bigger and better things.

WORD-OF-MOUTH CONNECTIONS

As with anywhere in the business world, some of the best jobs aren't advertised at all (like the one I just mentioned), so you need to sharpen your networking skills. Talk to your program director in residency or fellowship, or the chairperson of your department, and inquire about the residents and fellows who graduated before you. Where did they go? You have a common connection; you trained at the same place. With the internet and social media, it's easy enough to find someone—and nine times out of 10, if you reach out to them sincerely and authentically, they'll be willing to talk when they find out the common connection of med school or residency, etc. If you're fortunate, they might know people in their area who are looking for someone.

Your residency and fellowship program have a vested interest in you getting a job, in the sense that they want their data to look good. The amount of direct assistance you receive, however, is going to depend on a lot of other circumstances. If you're the standout resident in your department, sure, the chairperson might come up to you and volunteer to make a connection. But the reality is that they're also busy with their own lives and jobs, in terms of practicing medicine and teaching, so it may not be in the forefront of their mind.

Yet, the network is right there in front of you. Opportunities will be there every day. The question is, can you recognize them? And if you do, what are you going to do about it? One good way of thinking about it: Everyone loves to give their opinion. Simply asking someone in your department what they think about a given hospital or region might yield a negative or positive comment, and then it's up to you to sort it out.

You can expand this strategy by searching hospital websites in your desired region and researching staff bios. You're looking for any possible connection—where they went to college, trained, did a fellowship, or practiced—and simply reaching out to learn if they're aware of any openings or colleagues who might be able to help. Of course, this kind of cold call is a tougher road than a direct referral, but you never know what doors you might potentially open.

STEP OUTSIDE YOUR COMFORT ZONE

I was in my first job and looking to change—yes, I was among the 60% of physicians who change their first job within the first two years. I had my sights on another orthopedic group in town and figured out with some research that one of the two senior partners used to work for my then-current employer. My thought bubble was: "Well, there's a reason that guy left. I wonder if it's same reason I'm thinking of leaving." Sure enough, when I called him, he knew exactly why I was looking to make a change.

He wasn't the sole decision maker, however. I learned through the grapevine that the other partner was doing some consulting work for a medical device company that I was too, and that we'd both be at the same conference dinner. I didn't care about the conference. I didn't care about the dinner. I had one objective, and that was to make a connection. I didn't know anybody there, so I followed him around like a little puppy, off to the side. When it came time to sit for dinner, the moment he sat down, I snagged the seat right next to him and introduced myself. Two weeks later, I'd been hired as the newest member of the group.

Vetting Your Options

Anybody who has or is about to embark on a career in medicine has put in the time and effort. You wouldn't have finished residency if you hadn't busted your butt. You've also delayed gratification, at least from an economic perspective, compared to many of your peers in other industries. As a result, it can be easy to look at the dollar signs that somebody is dangling in front of you—but you need to ask the right questions to find out what a job is going to entail.

BENEFITS

You're so ready to be done with school and training, and ready to finally make some decent money, that perhaps you're not even thinking or caring about benefits. Even so, you'll want to know the basics such as vacation, sick time, and whether there's a 401(k) or other retirement plan. Assuming health insurance is offered, can your spouse get on the plan? How much do you pay versus what they pay as your employer? Do they provide disability coverage, including occupation-specific disability coverage? Do you get an allowance for continuing medical education? Depending on where you work and the state you live in, that could cost thousands of dollars a year.

RESPONSIBILITIES

Whether you're on a phone call with a recruiter, or interviewing with a decision maker who's a physician or in HR, these are just a few of the items you will want to know:

- How many days a week am I going to have to do clinic?

- Is there ER call? If so, how many hospitals?

- If you're in a surgical field, how many half days or full days a week am I going to be operating potentially?

- Will I have any administrative responsibilities? If so, what do they entail?

BONUS STRUCTURE

I'll confess, I didn't know what overhead was when I was finishing residency—and if it was taught in med school, I must've been playing hooky that day. In simple accounting terms, it's everything your employer needs to pay to keep the enterprise running: administrative staff, rent, A/C, lights, water and sewer. As an employee, they will be allocating a certain percentage of their overhead against your usage—so you may not even qualify for a bonus until you hit your overhead number, which includes your salary and in some cases your malpractice insurance (which can be a huge chunk of change!). If they don't spell it out for you, it's imperative to ask: "What does my overhead consist of?"

NON-COMPETE CLAUSES

A lot of employers will include non-compete clauses in your contract, so you want to understand the implications. Think about it from their perspective: "If I employ you and you're going to leave, my assumption is that you've generated a book of business, have some intimate knowledge of the area, and may be taking patients with you." In most cases, they will be defined by geography, such as a certain mile radius. There are a lot of nuances to such clauses and their enforceability, however—so this is most certainly a time to have your health-care attorney explain to you exactly what you're signing, or how it might be negotiable.

Interviewing Beyond the Basics

Interviews aren't just an opportunity for the prospective employer to find out about you. Even more important, I would argue, is for you to ask the questions to find out about them.

LET'S SEE THE BOOKS

You can't just go to Google or AI and find the accounting books for a private practice or hospital. But nothing stops you from asking the person you're interviewing with, or the HR contact, to show you the books. For perspective, this isn't about the numbers; it's about determining their transparency.

I have more than a few colleagues who regret not doing this. In one instance, the employer had not been clear about the metrics or formula for overhead, which meant that my friend didn't qualify for a bonus. Even though he'd worked more hours and brought in more revenue than some of his peers, it didn't matter—he didn't have anything in writing about the overhead metrics or how he could actually earn a bonus. When he pressed the issue, he was simply told, "It's complicated." By then, it was too late, and he ultimately left the job.

When you ask about the books there are a few possible outcomes. They might say yes or no, and it may come down to policy, but their facial expression and tone will speak volumes. At an interview for one of my private practice jobs, I even had a managing partner voluntarily say, "We're very interested in you, let me know when you can come in to see the books." That told me everything I needed to know about him as an individual and them as a group.

If you do get to see the books, or a redacted version of them, what are you looking for? For starters:

- How many patient visits do they have monthly/annually?

- What is their monthly/annual revenue?

- What is their overhead percentage—and how much is going to get allocated towards you?

That final bullet is key. If their overhead runs at 75% and you're bringing in $100,000 in revenue, those fixed costs only leave $25,000. That's not efficient. You want to get a sense not just about what kind of doctors these people are, but how the ship is being run.

If you're looking at a partnership, you will also want to find out what the buy-in is, and what the metrics and timeline are. Ask how they came up with the dollar amount for the buy-in and what you get in exchange. Is it just furniture or legitimate physical assets (X-ray, MRI, etc.)? You don't want to wait until you're working with them to find out these critical pieces of information.

A larger hospital system may have legal reasons that prevent them from disclosing the full books. But that doesn't stop you from asking. Again, the tone of the response should tell you a lot. Moreover, if they're really interested in you, they ought to be able to say, "While I can't show you the actual books, because you're not a member of this hospital system yet, I'd be happy to once you are on board. But in the meantime, understand that our overhead runs somewhere between 40% and 53%." They didn't give you the exact number, but it gives you an idea—and they ought to know that off the top of their head without actually looking it up.

DO YOUR OWN REFERENCE CHECK

A potential employer will ask you for references. Part of your due diligence should be to do a reference check of your own! If you are planning to join a practice, you can strategically contact people who can vouch for the ability, personality, character, and ethics of key people at the organization. If it's a surgical practice, the charge nurse at a surgery center or hospital OR will know all the dirt. "Hi, I'm Dr. Smith, and I'm thinking about moving to the Minneapolis area and joining Dr. Jones' group. I know you don't know me, but I'm trying to do some due diligence. What's it like to work with him? Is he good at what he does? Does he throw stuff in the OR, or does he yell? Would you go to him as a patient?"

One of two things is going to happen. If they think very highly of Dr. Jones, the charge nurse has absolutely zero reason to not tell you, because nothing's going to come back to bite them in the rear. If they pause or say, "Look, I'm not sure I'm at liberty to answer that," you have your answer in an indirect way.

This tactic isn't restricted to the surgical field. For example, if you're looking for a job in pediatrics or dermatology, talk to other pediatricians or dermatologists in the area or to some referring docs.

ONLINE REVIEWS

These can be another data point, but take them with a grain of salt, because you can't please everybody. With a doctor who has 100 reviews and 99 of them are glowing, you can probably bet that outlier was on the patient's end. In addition, it's worth reading some of the comments that people leave. Are they all just 5 stars, or are there certain comments that resonate with the type of person you are or physician you want to be? For example, "Dr. X really listens and doesn't make me feel rushed" could be a positive indicator of their personal style.

This is your life. You spent all this time getting here. Why not try your best to do it right?

Analyzing Your Options

Once you start to get the lay of the land as far as possible job options, it behooves you to be proactive and do your homework. Let's use the US Medical Licensing Exam as an example, whether you've taken it yet or not. Do you study for it? Of course you do. So why would you not invest the same effort into your first job?

My favorite tool for doing this is borrowed from the business world: a SWOT analysis. What are the Strengths of that job? What are the Weaknesses? What are the Opportunities? What are the Threats?

As an example, let's consider geographic region. When I was starting out, I wanted to be west of the Mississippi, and interviewed for jobs in the San Francisco Bay Area, down through Los Angeles, and over into parts of Texas. I had a couple of offers in the Bay Area, but then I considered supply and demand. A lot of people want to live there, which probably means lots of competition and a high cost of living. How many years would it take to establish my practice against physicians who were already entrenched? In contrast, at the time, the Phoenix metro area was experiencing a population boom. (And it still is.) Although I assumed there was a base of established orthopedic surgeons, it seemed like a better opportunity based purely on demographics. So, San Francisco went into the Weakness bucket, and Phoenix into Strength and Opportunity.

You could also incorporate geography in the sense of working in a city versus practicing rural medicine. And if you want to do a deeper dive, do some research to get a sense of whether a given area might need your specialty, or if it's already saturated. If there's a shortage somewhere relative to population, that might be a tick mark in the Strength column even if it's not your first choice in where you want to live.

In business terms, the Threat box is usually defined as a competitive threat—but in the medical world, the more important aspect is the perceived threat you represent to other physicians. You're the newbie, moving into essentially what is somebody else's backyard. Say you are a surgeon moving into a new town. Do you join the same group as a specialist with a great reputation and 20 years' experience in the hopes of inheriting that practice when they retire? Or do you strategically try to establish your footprint on the other side of the city, realizing that it may be a long commute? There's no right or wrong answer.

Another item to plug into a SWOT analysis is if you have a significant other or are in a seriously committed relationship. Their happiness is going to play a role in your happiness and success, including not only their personality and location preference, but their career path. If your significant other is fresh out of college with a marketing degree, it's going to be a tough road for them to build a book of business in a town with 3,000 people. Even if the ultimate dream is to live a rural lifestyle, a first job in a bigger city might make sense while you both get established. This extends to the rest of your family too. If you really enjoy hanging out with parents and siblings who live in Boston, setting up your practice in Boise is going to limit how often you see them.

Example SWOT Analysis

STRENGTHS	WEAKNESSES
– Already have my medical license in that state – Quality of life: hiking/biking/skiing/fishing – Close to my spouse's family – Familiar from having vacationed here	– Cost of living – Far from my family – Unsure of business options for spouse – Probably a long commute
OPPORTUNITIES	THREATS
– Young, fast-growing population – Nearby medical device & pharma HQs – Lots of real estate investment options	– Web search indicates my specialty is highly competitive – Healthcare system dominated by one hospital system

Your Work Doesn't Stop with the Offer (a.k.a., Read the Fine Print)

You've got a solid offer that checks enough of the right SWOT boxes? Great! There's an old saying that someone who serves as their own attorney has a fool for a client, and that's true when it comes to reviewing the legalese in employment contracts. It's worth every penny to get an opinion from an attorney who specializes in healthcare, because even if it's in plain English, the law often comes down to interpretation. I've seen too many physicians get trapped because they didn't do their due diligence, or they hired a friend who's an attorney in a different field. You've already spent hundreds of thousands of dollars to go through medical school, why not invest a few thousand to get someone who's qualified to protect your interests?

While you're asking the healthcare attorney, from a legal perspective, what the holes are in the contract, don't stop there. Due diligence can also include people in the community who you might know, people who already work at that place, or your chairperson or faculty from residency or fellowship. If you've spent three to seven years with these folks, I guarantee you at least one of them would be happy to review your contract with you. Ask them if the terms are realistic from a practice perspective, whether it is salary range, time off, or the required patient visits to hit your numbers. Keep in mind, all of them have been in the same position as you and will have a better perspective on the medical aspects than even the healthcare attorney. Moreover, the odds are good that they're among the aforementioned 60% of docs-who-left-jobs in under two years and learned from their own mistakes.

Everything in this world is negotiable, including contracts and details of salary and work responsibilities. Just because an HR person says X doesn't mean it has to be X. Ask for Y, and what's the worst that can happen? They'll say, "Sorry, we can't do that."

A QUICK WORD ABOUT RED FLAGS

Say you're looking for a job in a specialty journal or on a website, and you spot an ad that looks like this:

BE/BC[5] RADIATION ONCOLOGIST, Laredo, Texas hospital arrangement, $1 million first-year guaranteed. 956-555-1212 or email jobs@docjobbs.com

"A million bucks!" you say to yourself. "Where do I sign up? I've been making $33,000 a year for the past five years and have a ton of medical school debt that I'd love to wipe out."

If it sounds too good to be true, alas, it probably is. So, let's apply a SWOT analysis. Do you know where Laredo is, and do you want to live there for a year or longer? Do you understand what happens after that first year? Is this a paycheck that you get and that money is yours... or is there fine print somewhere that the ad doesn't say? In all likelihood, a deal like this has some hidden hazards. I've seen it happen to colleagues:

- After year one, you're on an eat-what-you-kill basis—which is to say, take that first year, grow your practice, then revenue minus overhead is yours. But going into it, you don't know the overhead, nor what the scope of growth might be.

---

5   If you're clueless like I was at that early stage in my career, that acronym stands for Board Eligible/Board Certified.

- They've thrown out a cool million to hook you and get you in the door. Are you going to go from $1 million in year one to $100,000 in year two? Because that's the actual footprint that you can serve and the money you potentially earn.

- In year two, you realize this isn't what you signed up for. (Well, technically it is.) It's way less than what you thought you would make. You're not practicing the type of medicine you thought you were going to, because the demographics are different from what you believed. You're doing something you don't want to be doing in a place you don't want to live. You decide you'd rather pick up stakes and move to Charlotte, North Carolina.

- Not so fast, my friend, as Lee Corso used to say on ESPN's College GameDay: The contract you signed agreed to a five-year stint. Short of that, the year-one $1 million was an interest-free loan, not a salary, and you owe it back. Unless you socked all seven figures away in an interest-bearing account for safekeeping, you're in a bind.

Is this an extreme example? Sure. But the reality is, the harder it is for a place to get people there, the more they need to incentivize—which usually means money. Did you really think that as a new, inexperienced physician, somebody thought you were worth $1 million?

You Don't Know What You Don't Know

In the introduction, I noted a statistic that most physicians coming into the workforce currently are at their first job for less than two years. Now, you may not fall into that category, but it's still important for perspective. You don't have to hit a home run the first time you're at the plate. No matter what you do, a job may not be the right fit and you may not know until you get there. Did you know what med school was going to be like before you took your first class? Did you know how much work it was going to be? Did you know what residency was going to be like until you started it? No, no, and no.

People can give you all the advice they want, but until you step through that door, it's a mystery. Sure, there's a chance you've landed your dream job and you'll be there for a decade. But if you don't do your homework, you've skyrocketed the odds of being unhappy. In contrast, if you have prepared yourself mentally, you will learn in that process—both what to do and what not to do, creating options as you sketch out your roadmap to something bigger, better, or different. ***Chance favors the prepared mind.***

PRACTICE PEARLS
Psychology Tips to be the Physician that Colleagues and Patients Love

Sometime when you're bored, ask your friends and family how many physicians they know who have good bedside manner. Then, when you really want to get an earful, ask another physician what they really think about the traits of their most difficult colleagues.

Over the years, I've observed and collected what I call "pearls": little bits of wisdom on the art of dealing with people that have helped me be a better physician to my patients and a better teammate to my peers. In each chapter, I'll share a different pearl.

Take a seat. When you enter an examination room to consult with a patient, you have options. You can stand at the door with your hand on the doorknob because you have a busy 40-patient clinic day. I get it. But realize the message you're conveying to that patient, to whom you owe your 100% undivided attention: "Can you get on with this?" You're not living in the moment, you're living in the next moment. Psychologically, taking your hand off the doorknob puts you in the top 10%. If you walk to the other end of the room, opposite the door, you'll be in the 5%. Sit down on that side of the room, and congratulations, you made it into the 1%. Even better, sit on a chair or stool that's lower than the exam table, and you're letting the patient feel like they're in charge—and shifting the dynamics of the room.

CHAPTER 2

Physician, Know Thyself

*Choosing a Practice Model
that Works for You*

THE OLD SAYING IS THAT practice makes perfect. But there's no such thing as a perfect practice model—everything comes with pros, cons, and tradeoffs. Being smart in the beginning, and knowing yourself, will help you understand what you need to do to keep your options open.

EMPLOYEE MODEL

The most common first step in a medical career is as an employee of a healthcare system, hospital, or private practice. This model offers a number of advantages for the newly minted MD or DO, allowing you to gain experience and focus on patient care while your employer handles the administrative details of billing, staffing, and running an office. On the financial side, employment comes first and foremost with a predictable income (which can help with paying off your school loans), as well as benefits packages that include health insurance, sick time, and paid vacation. If you're fortunate, your employer may offer some form of profit sharing as well.

The downside of the employee model is relative lack of freedom: Your employer will dictate how many people you need to see, the hours you work, how much ER call you take, and how many days off you get each year. It's also not risk-free. Remember that stat from the introduction chapter about how many physicians leave their job in less than two years? Nothing is forever, and there's a good chance you may be one of them.

The bottom line: Do you just want to be given patients and paid a salary, while not dealing with the nitty-gritty aspects of business and administration? Then the employee model may be right for you.

ACADEMIC

Beyond being a community practitioner, whether it's private practice or an employee model, an academic setting is yet another option: helping to teach med students, residents, and fellows. By virtue of going through residency or as an intern, you've likely already had some exposure to teaching, in the form of a med student rotating with you and following you around like a shadow. Either by them observing you interact with a patient or an actual didactic, here's-what-you-do-in-this-situation discussion, they are absorbing and learning. You may not view it that way in the moment, because you're just trying to get through residency, but you've been taught and you're teaching along the way. By the end of your stint, you probably have a good idea whether teaching is for you—or if you just want to see patients and go home at the end of the day.

The academic category also includes doing research your-self, either as a focused pursuit or hybrid along with teaching and/or clinical work.

PRIVATE PRACTICE

Private practice isn't dead, but there are certainly fewer private practitioners around today than there used to be. There are a variety of reasons for that, and the simplest is that it's harder to make the math work. As insurance reimbursements continue to trend downward, your ability to command a better rate is next to zero because the carrier determines your contract. Meanwhile, overhead is trending up: rent or mortgage payments for your office space; salaries for your medical assistant, front desk, and backroom folks who handle calls and appointments, administrators, and techs; medical malpractice insurance; plus, utilities, maintenance, and everything else.

Nonetheless, there are those who are still able to navigate the system and embrace the optionality that private practice can deliver. The advantages of being your own boss are well known: making your own schedule, the potential to make more money, and the ability to write off things like office space, your car, and other expenses.

But those advantages also come with tradeoffs. Making that work is a matter of several factors, including your area of specialty. I would argue, for example, that it's a little easier for a surgeon or dermatologist to bob, weave, and utilize other avenues than it might be for a pediatrician. Perhaps most important, going into private practice requires the interest and aptitude for running a business, in addition to managing the day-to-day medical tasks.

Do you have to be business savvy? Not necessarily. But if you're not, and you still don't want to be employed by a big hospital system or a big group, then you had better surround yourself with people who do know their stuff. An NFL team might hire a 30-year-old to be their head coach, because they're innovative and creative, and can tap into aspects of football that the current 68-year-old head coaches aren't able to see and think and do. But at the same time, that youngster hasn't experienced certain aspects of coaching at the pro level, so it can help to have seasoned vets as offensive and defensive coordinators to guide their ingenuity.

In the same way, if you're new and you want to take this on, you need to surround yourself with a team that has the skills and experience to make it work. Note, that doesn't necessarily mean employing a bunch of high-paid people right out of the box. Perhaps you have a medical assistant and an administrator who handles your internal office dealings, and separately you retain the services of a healthcare business consultant as an independent contractor. Some of them are doctors who've been there, done that, others are pure businesspeople who know how to market and operate an organization.

Like most things in life, you get what you pay for and if something sounds too good to be true, it probably is. You run across someone who claims 25 years' of experience in healthcare consulting. They tell you they can grow your practice, do marketing and search engine optimization on your website, and get you a better healthcare contract with Blue Cross, all for a total of $2,500. Even at a glance, even if you don't have any business experience, that sounds ridiculous. But what if they said $10,000 or $25,000? Maybe that's a good deal, maybe it isn't. The devil is in the details, and it's incumbent upon you to sift through and discover what's legit. The good news for today's doctor is that the internet gives you a tool that previous generations didn't have; the bad news is that it's also given birth to a lot of predatory companies trying to prey on unwitting victims.

If your route in private practice leads you to a potential

partnership in a group, that comes with its own set of variables. What are the metrics, and are they based on a timeline or revenues? What, if anything, will the buy-in be? Some groups are notorious for churning and burning, getting you in the door only to discover there's really no viable track to partnership. Moreover, you need to do the math on the economic value. What are you getting out of being a partner? If the buy-in is $100,000, does that mean you have partial ownership in the furniture, or the revenues from imaging and the surgery center? If it's $1 million, can that even possibly pencil out? A final word of advice: If you're offered partnership, whatever the buy-in might be, don't take out a loan unless you're getting a 0% interest rate.

LOCUM TENENS

Moving around a lot doesn't necessarily mean you have a fear of commitment. For physicians who also enjoy traveling, locum tenens work allows them to embrace the nomadic side of medicine. Doing short stints in different cities or towns might mean that you have a little less control over what you're doing and when you're doing it, and you'll need to be licensed in the states where you practice, but there can be several upsides for the effort. The pay is usually pretty good, you get to see different parts of the state or country, and the employer will usually cover your malpractice insurance. For those who embrace the lifestyle, it can be a good fit.

This doesn't have to be an all-or-nothing proposition, either. I have a number of colleagues who do a majority of their practice in their home state, then they'll pick a multiweek period where they're going to do some locums work—and enjoy the recreational or cultural benefits of the destination during their downtime. Important: If you're employed, you'll need to clear it with your employer that you not only get the time off but can potentially have a separate source of income. (Ideally coming to you rather than them.) But you need to ask *and* get it in writing.

HYBRID

The most common variant of the hybrid approach is what's known as a Physician Services Agreement (PSA). In simple terms, this is a contract between you (with or without a physician group) and a healthcare entity or hospital. The PSA is basically a pseudo-private practice model, which allows you to still basically remain in private practice while leveraging the benefits of a hospital contract. (More on this topic in chapter 5.) In order for this to be an attractive relationship, they will want to look at your last few years of data—which means it's not something you can approach as a freshly minted doctor. Once you've been in practice for a couple of years, you can show how busy you've been, how many patients you've seen, and how much revenue you might bring in.

The Challenge of Course Correction

There are advantages and disadvantages to every practice model, depending on the route you take. If you go down path A, does that mean you can't move over to path B later? Absolutely not. People change all the time.

Although none of the options is a one-way street, some of them may be more difficult to navigate. If you're in private practice, you can make the transition to being an employee, benefiting from a steady paycheck while realizing the loss of freedom is going to sting. Conversely, changing course from an employee to being your own boss might be more lucrative, but it's also going to be a shock, given all of the additional business responsibilities and uncertainties.

Once you have taken the academic route, however, making a move to a private practice can be a much bigger challenge. As an analogy, imagine you've been teaching something very specialized such as pediatric hematology oncology for 15 years, and now I'm going to make you take a board exam in general pediatrics—the stuff that you knew everything about when you finished residency. But since your fellowship, you haven't seen a kid with an ear infection or an infant with scoliosis. I don't know about you, but that'd be daunting for me. Again, conversely, a doctor in a private-practice role is going to have at least an initial struggle going from seeing and treating patients to teaching fellows and residents who are going to be asking about or doing research on the broader scope of medicine.

None of these switches are impossible if you're committed to making it work, but you need to be aware: The longer you've followed the same roadmap, the more you're typecast in a role.

PRACTICE PEARL
Redirect, Don't Interrupt

The internet comes with a whole lot of pluses and minuses, and the one physicians feel most acutely is patients who have done their own "research." Rather than interrupting, learn how to redirect them: "Jane, I hear what you're saying about that, but you just mentioned something else that caught my attention, because I actually think that's really relevant to why you're here." When we allow ourselves to listen, we can assimilate information in a way that can be used to improve the way we practice—and let patients know we have their best interests in mind.

43

No one likes a lazy person.

—DR. AMIT SAHASRABUDHE

____

CHAPTER 3

No Excess Baggage

License Now for Optionality Later

ONE OF THE BEST INSIGHTS I've ever received was from my orthopedic trauma chair during residency: *When you're a resident, that's the least amount of baggage you'll ever have in your life from a medical practice standpoint.* You're protected under the umbrella of your attendings and the university or community hospital. Once you get out into the real world and the buck stops with you, the baggage starts accruing. Patients are yours now. You can't please everybody. Nothing can stop somebody from making a claim or an accusation, and you need to deal with it, whether it's valid or not.

This has important unseen implications down the road. Someone files a complaint against you with the Alabama medical board, but they decide that it's frivolous and drop it with no action. Years later, you're applying for a license in Georgia—and one of the questions is, "Have you ever had a board complaint?" Well, now you need to answer "Yes," and explain that it was dropped. Probably no big deal, but it still could be a hurdle. (If the complaint was ruled legitimate, it would definitely be an issue.) Depending on the state and its licensing paperwork verbiage, a complaint may stay on your record for several years or forever. Above all, the longer you're in practice, the more your exposure multiplies.

The Antidote: Diversify Your Portfolio of Licenses

In my professional opinion, it's prudent to retain at least three active state medical licenses at any given time. If something goes sideways in your main practice in California—even if you've done nothing wrong!—you have ready-to-go back-up plans in Oregon and Washington. Someone is always going to need you, and you'll be able to keep a roof over your head and put food on the table. While it might be easy to get a job, however, it's harder to get the medical license if you have baggage.

When you earn your medical training license, you don't really have much choice—it will be dictated by the state where you're doing your internship and/or residency. Once you're a resident or fellow and have passed the US Medical Licensing Exam (USMLE) step three, however, it's time to think more broadly. At that point, you can get your MD or DO license to practice medicine in any state—technically you could hang up your own shingle even if you quit residency.

Expanding your range of licenses requires asking similar questions to what we addressed in chapter 1 and the SWOT analysis. Where could you see yourself living or practicing? How important is it to be close to your family, or to where you or your significant other grew up? Is it possible you'll need to help care for aging parents in the future? You don't need to limit yourself to those criteria, and there's no sense in adding licenses just for the sake of collecting them; there needs to be a strategic reason.

For example, having multiple licenses also gives you optionality in ancillary medicine and alternatives to seeing patients, including expert witness work. That's why I added Alaska and Utah to my license arsenal. Even though I couldn't envision a permanent move to either place, both offer the allure of outdoor activities that I enjoy such as mountain biking and hiking, so I can double dip. I'll address these topics in more detail in chapter 6 and 7, so stay tuned.

At the risk of sounding like an old guy claiming he had to walk to school uphill both ways through three feet of snow, physicians today have an advantage. Gone are the days where you had to apply individually to each state, with applications up to 25 pages, and having to round up and submit transcripts from residency and med school. Nowadays, there's something called an Interstate Medical Licensure Compact (IMLC): a central website that you fill out information on, and then participating states rely on your home state to verify that your license is in good standing before licensing you in theirs. As of the time that this book is being published, not all states participate in the compact, but more and more are doing it. There's a handy map right on the home page of the IMLC that shows the U.S. states and their current level of participation: https://imlcc.com.

2026 USA Interstate Medical Licensure Compact (IMLC) Participants

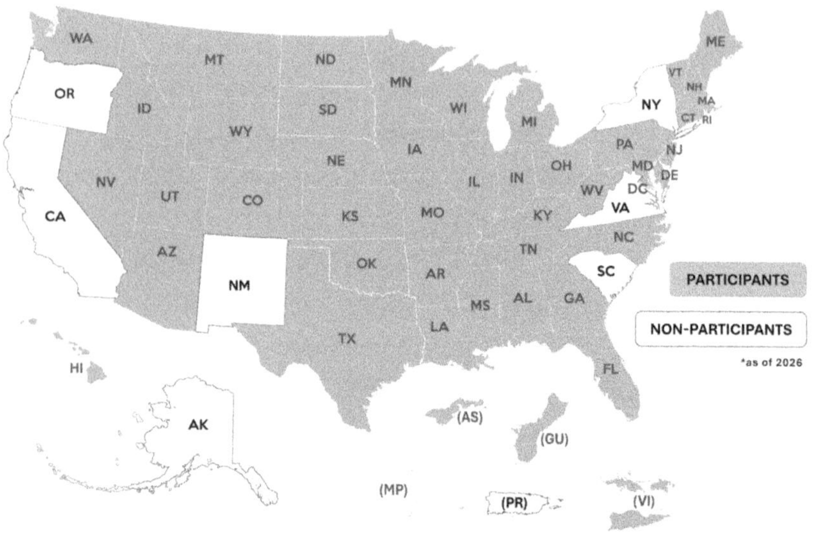

The above map shows all states that participate at some level as of 2026 shaded in dark gray. Please see the IMLC website or consult individual state boards for the most up-to-date information.

PRACTICE PEARL

Connecting with Patients at their Level

It's common for a physician to make some notations on arthroscopy photos for a patient to help them understand what they're seeing, but Dr. Dan Guttman showed me the value of taking things to the next level. In his post-arthroscopy photos, he'd draw a few arrows to critical areas, and label the finding, then at the bottom of the final slide, he'd use a Sharpie to draw a smiley face. I asked him why. He looked at me and said, "Before you were a resident, would you have had any idea what you were looking at? No. So a patient certainly won't. But what's something that everyone universally understands? A smiley face. That lets the patient know that I was happy with how the surgery went." From that day forward, I incorporated that technique for every patient.

CHAPTER 4

Insurance 101

Protecting Yourself, Now and in the Future

THIS CHAPTER IS FOCUSED ON the down-and-dirty basics: health insurance, life insurance, disability insurance, auto insurance, homeowners insurance, cyber insurance, and medical malpractice insurance—and also an exotic variant called captive insurance that will eventually come on your radar. (We'll be discussing the insurance that pays you when you see patients in the next chapter.)

Your first question might be: How do these common types of insurance, other than malpractice, mean something different to me as a physician than they do to anyone else?

The short answer is that, simply by virtue of your chosen career, you aren't exactly flying below the radar. You're more likely than the average Joe and Sally to have a big home, a nice car, and other valuable assets. All of that adds up to exposure.

Keep in mind, circumstances can be very different for your situation now than as it evolves in the future. For now, I'm simply introducing these topics so that you're aware of them to strategically protect yourself, your family, and your financial well-being as much as you can. The main recommendation that I can give is to consult with experts, which could include a broker who specializes in insurance for high-net-worth individuals, a CPA, a financial advisor, and even a lawyer. As they say in the car ads, "Your mileage may vary."

So let's get to it.

HOMEOWNERS, AUTO, AND UMBRELLA INSURANCE

If you own a home, you're familiar with homeowners insurance because the bank wouldn't have allowed you to take out a mortgage without it. Same with insurance on your vehicles. The dealer wants confirmation that you have it—not for your protection, but because they're giving you a loan.

On an individual level, those two types of insurance provide you protection as well, to whatever extent you choose. But beyond that, and speaking in general terms, most physicians will want a sturdier shield. That's where an umbrella policy comes in: an added layer of liability protection beyond the limits of your auto and home policies.

LIFE INSURANCE

At the risk of radically oversimplifying a dizzyingly complex industry, there are two main categories of life insurance to consider: term life and whole life.

- Think of term life insurance as renting a house. You are paying money every month and not getting anything back for it, unless you die. Technically, if you die, you yourself aren't getting anything for it, your beneficiaries are. Term life is the cheaper of the two to procure.

- Whole life premiums are generally more expensive, but there are a few reasons for that. First, you are paying a premium towards a death benefit, just as with term life. But second, part of the premium goes towards cash value in the policy, which increases every year.

As a result, which type you choose and when, is very situation dependent. When I first started practicing, my wife and I had minimal money, debt in our first home, and two cars with loans. At the time, it made the most sense for me to have a term life policy that would ensure she was OK if I passed away unexpectedly. The nuance, though, was that it was a policy that could be converted to whole life once we could afford it—with the side benefit that it didn't require an additional medical exam. (Remember the discussion about baggage and medical licenses? Same thing applies in insurance: Your premium is more likely to be more expensive when you're older than when you're fresh out of training and have minimal health baggage!)

Eventually I converted that plan into a whole life policy. My premium went up, but I started building cash value. Without getting too into the weeds, there were two key provisions: The cash value growth was tied to the S&P 500, with a cap on the upside if the market went up a lot, but also a guaranteed gain of 2% even if it went down. Second, the cash value would allow me to take out a loan against the policy tax free. The reason I chose to get that policy was tied to my plans to retire at age 50. I knew I couldn't pull money out of my retirement funds (IRA and 401(k)), at least without a penalty, and so that policy would offer a buffer if I needed cash for whatever reason. As noted earlier, an insurance broker or your financial advisor can provide more precise recommendations for your situation and the math involved.

HEALTH INSURANCE

News flash: Healthcare costs keep going up. Given your chosen profession, you're also well aware of the importance of having insurance to mitigate that. As with all types of insurance, there are a dizzying array of policy types, from bare bones to gold plated—and every choice you make has implications for your coverage and deductibles.

My own bias, whether you get health insurance on your own or through your employer, is to have a policy that is HSA (health savings account) eligible, and if you're young and healthy, to consider a high-deductible plan because the probability of needing expensive care is lower—why pay more in premium than you need to? Your situation may be different, but here's how I played it:

- I maxed out the money I was putting into my HSA account.

- When I had health expenses, I didn't use the HSA—I paid them out of pocket. If I decided later to pay myself back out of the HSA, I kept the receipts so that would still be an option.

- By letting that account grow, both with the additional contributions plus the compound interest, that account grew rapidly.

Here's the reason why I did it this way: Having an HSA is like a supercharged IRA for health expenses. (We'll talk more about IRAs and investing in chapter 9, but stick with me here.) When you're old and gray, don't have a steady income, healthcare costs have gone up, and you're no longer on an employer's plan, an HSA provides a nice source of funds. But the tax advantages are what make it so unusual: When you sock money away into an HSA, you get a tax deduction on the front end. But even better, when you take money out, there isn't tax on the withdrawal or your gains either as long as the funds are spent on a healthcare expense. As of the time I'm writing this, there isn't a better deal around, in my opinion. Let's hope Congress keeps it that way.

Part of my reason for choosing to save rather than spend my HSA funds is that I planned to retire early, long before I was eligible for Medicare. I knew my wife and I needed to cover ourselves for a decade or more before Uncle Sam swooped in. Taking a "plan for the worst, hope for the best" approach can help you navigate long-term situations, whether or not they actually happen. You're not just getting health care for this month; you're trying to do what's right for you well into the future.

DISABILITY INSURANCE

Let's say you're a dermatologist who does in-office procedures, you badly injure one of your hands doing yardwork over the weekend, and it's serious enough to prevent you from doing procedures for the foreseeable future. Can you still be a dermatologist? Could you be a non-procedural dermatologist, who only evaluates patients and then refers them to colleagues for procedures?

This line of questioning is essential to understanding the difference between a general disability policy and an occupation-specific policy. If I, as a surgeon, lost the ability to use my hands to operate and only had regular disability insurance, the carrier could deny paying coverage, because I could still (theoretically) become a motivational speaker, med school professor, or Walmart greeter.

I realized I've kind of stacked the deck here with my analogy, but I believe you can see my point: General disability coverage is fine as far as it goes, but to truly protect yourself, occupation-specific disability insurance may be worth the extra expense.

That said, do not expect either kind of disability policy to pay out without a fight, because the game has changed a lot in recent years. In the past, lots of physicians went on disability, saying they couldn't work anymore because they had back pain—with little or no substantiation. They got paid out, only for the system to learn that many of them were basically frivolous. Now there's additional scrutiny and a more significant burden of proof for a successful claim.

A few years ago, I had a surgical colleague who had been treated for cancer. Due to one of the side effects from radiation and chemo, he ended up dislocating a shoulder, resulting in one of his arms in a sling and a long stint in rehab. As a physician, you can imagine the difficulty of operating with only one hand—but even the occupation-specific disability carrier fought tooth and nail against paying. After running him through multiple evaluations and reviewing plenty of documentation, the company eventually relented.

A few other important nuances to disability insurance:

- It's cheapest to procure when you are in med school, because you are young and don't have any baggage, but you can't get occupation-specific coverage at that point. Once you have decided on a specialty, your residency program may have some options to consider if you don't want to shop around on your own with a broker.

- There are potential tax implications that you will want to discuss with your CPA. Disability coverage should be procured with post-tax dollars, paid out of pocket not written off as a business expense. As of the most current rules, in the event of becoming disabled, that would allow your monthly payout to be tax-free. If you expensed your premiums, the payout would be taxed.

- Unlike car insurance and life insurance, disability policies are generally more expensive for women, due to childbirth being among the most common causes of becoming disabled.

MEDICAL MALPRACTICE INSURANCE

I'll admit, this is one of my least favorite aspects of being a physician. But, like the old saying about death and taxes being inevitable, so is malpractice coverage in medicine. An employer won't let you work somewhere without having it, a surgery center won't let you have privileges without seeing your malpractice certificate and what the coverage is, and so on. It's just part of the deal.

If there's any good news, it's that most malpractice claims are frivolous, and they get dropped because there's just no substance to them. There are a variety of benchmarks that must be met for a malpractice claim to have legs—but in the interest of brevity, I'll just encourage you to research that on your own.

Knowing that malpractice coverage is a necessity, it's worth building a folio of information by asking residents, fellows, attendings, or other seasoned physicians before you need to procure it on your own after residency/fellowship.

- When the time comes, it makes sense to start your search with the American Medical

Association, which has numerous options in different insurance categories.

- Some carriers only cover certain states, so ensure you have coverage in every state where your activities require it.

- If you prefer to DIY it, you certainly can do a web search, but in the interest of saving time and effort, a broker might be the better play. They can compare different carriers and options and put together a package that makes sense for your individual situation and the states you plan to practice in.

- Some carriers have regional or multi-state co-ops that are physician owned. The entity I used for most of my career, MICA (Mutual Insurance Company of Arizona), offers policies in Arizona, Colorado, Nevada, and Utah—but when I started to do expert witness work in Alaska, I used a broker to find an appropriate policy.

Malpractice coverage premiums are contingent on three primary factors:

- What your specialty is. For example, a primary care physician will likely have malpractice premiums that are less than an orthopedic surgeon or OB/GYN, because the risk is lower. However, a primary care physician who has been sued 20 times and lost 10 times is going to see their premiums skyrocket, if they can even get someone to insure them.

- How much baggage you have or don't have. Your premium is likely to be the lowest when you come out of residency and fellowship, and then steadily climb during the first five to seven years in practice. Your exposure is increasing, because every day, every week, every month, every year, you're seeing more new patients. Then there's the tail: the people who you saw yesterday, and let's say you never see them again. Depending on the state and its laws, there's an extended time frame during which that person can still file a claim against you.

- What state you work in. Malpractice premiums vary wildly from state to state, which is a function of the laws that are in place, how litigious the citizens are, and whether there is tort reform. Coverage in Pennsylvania, California, or New York tends to be more expensive than Arizona, while Texas has such serious tort reform that filing a successful malpractice claim is almost impossible. The Lone Star State caps the amount of dollars that an individual can get, and plaintiffs may find it difficult to even find an attorney willing to take their case.

An important side note: As an employee, you are somewhat safeguarded by virtue of working for some entity. If you are in private practice, however, there are additional precautionary measures to consider. If you were to practice under your name personally, you and your assets would be open to risk and exposure. So, part of the process is to form an LLC or a professional corporation (MD/DO PC) that does the practicing of medicine, including procuring your malpractice insurance.

One more item that they probably didn't tell you about in med school. Once you're done practicing, you're not done with paying for malpractice insurance, because you still have exposure to patients that you saw during the last few years of your career. You either need to have an active policy for as long as your state requires it or must purchase what is known as *tail insurance*. Some carriers may offer an option of a one-time lump sum that covers you through the tail period. Each one will have their own secret formula, but it comes down to a mix of your specialty, your claims history, and what you've paid in premiums over a certain time period. Still others may provide the tail coverage at no additional cost once you have been insured with them for a given duration.

In going through this process, I'll offer you a tip to keep in your pocket when you're approaching the end of your career. Here's what I discovered from a senior underwriter when she learned I was no longer going to be doing surgery or seeing patients in the office, but only doing independent medical exams (IMEs): I could get a malpractice premium that was less than 10% of my previous policy! If I had this coverage until age 55, my carrier would include my tail coverage at no additional cost. If I simply utilized this policy for three years, then decided to stop doing IMEs at that point, my lump sum tail coverage cost would be significantly less than it would have been when I was still doing surgeries.

BEST PRACTICES FOR MALPRACTICE

Insurance companies get a bad rap—sometimes deserved—but there's an important caveat here. The underwriters and the attorneys at your malpractice carrier are there to help you. They're an advisor, not an adversary. If a claim is being made, is being threatened, or even if a patient is acting a little squirrelly, pick up the phone and call your representative.

First and foremost, that ensures that they don't get blindsided, and you can explain to them what happened. They might even give you reassurance so that you're not up all night worrying about what kind of disaster you have on your hands. Second, they are the best people to guide you in your course of action. They may not be a physician, but they're a specialist in malpractice insurance, so you can assume they know how to navigate the situation. Trust me, they've seen it all.

In general, it simply makes sense to befriend your representatives. Even when there's no claim involved, they can answer questions about premiums, retirement, or anything else. You don't need to invite them over for Thanksgiving dinner, but who are they going to want to take care of first, someone who's curt and nasty, or someone who's kind and friendly?

On a related note: Malpractice coverage may be required by your employer, medical group, hospital system, or other entity, but experienced physicians will tell you: The best insurance policy is to act ethically, honestly, and professionally—not like a person that somebody wants to sue. Having good rapport and relationships with patients helps avoid issues with frivolous or hostile claims. It's OK to be wrong, and saying "I'm sorry" goes a long way.

CYBER INSURANCE

I'm old enough to remember when data breaches and ransomware attacks weren't part of the everyday lexicon. Unfortunately, a data-rich industry like healthcare makes a juicy target; I'd be willing to bet that you've personally experienced a breach notice as a patient within the healthcare system. If your practice stores personal health information such as medical records, test results, and medical bills, cyber insurance can help protect you against the steep fines from a HIPAA violation, and help you recover in case of a cyber incident.

CAPTIVE INSURANCE

Based on personal experience and situations I have heard about from peers, I am somewhat reticent to even raise this topic. But you're going to hear about it at some point, so let me just share what I know. Captive insurance is designed to provide coverage for possible outcomes that are either super expensive or impossible to get through traditional carriers. In simple terms, it's a shared risk pool on scenarios with a statistically low probability, with potential protective and financial benefits on the back end.

It's commonly used by auto dealers who want to insure against catastrophic events, such as the entire dealership burning to the ground or a supplier that shuts down. In the medical world, for example, you could take out a policy against the loss of a key employee who would be difficult, expensive, or impossible to replace. In 2019, you could have insured against a health-related scare that resulted in a nationwide shutdown of schools and businesses—if you catch my drift—though I bet the premiums to protect against that now would be astronomical.

Beyond any payouts for a claim, there can be tax advantages, such as the funds being subject to capital gains tax, as opposed to ordinary income tax. And there's an optionality piece, as far as being able to use the funds for other purposes once the captive money has been held for a specified period.

While this sounds like an interesting opportunity, there is no free lunch. Legislators and the IRS (which has a division that specializes in captive insurance) have heightened scrutiny on the practice in recent years, even for legitimate claims. As with any cautionary tale, you don't want to try to minimize one type of risk while inadvertently exposing yourself to another.

PRACTICE PEARL
Set Expectations

During my fellowship, I had a director who would tell his ACL patients in pre-op, "I just want to remind you that you're going to come out of this with the worst pain you've ever experienced." He saw my confused look when I heard him say that, and later on he explained. "I'm setting an expectation, but it's really a false expectation, because it will not be the worst pain they've ever experienced," he said. "It'll be painful, but when they compare it to all the other pain that they've had in their life, the probability of it being the worst is low. When that happens, it makes them feel like they chose a phenomenal surgeon."

CHAPTER 5

Contracts and Codes

The Two Cs of Getting Paid Properly

A FEW YEARS BACK, I had a group of physicians assistants rotating with me at my surgical practice. In addition to the medical teaching aspect, I'd often share insights about billing and coding, which eventually led to doing a lecture series at the school that they attended.

Make no mistake, coding and billing is inherently as dry and boring a topic as you're going to find. But on the first day of class, I'd tell them what I'll tell you now:

If you don't understand how to code properly, you might be leaving tens or hundreds of thousands of dollars on the table every single year.

In my experience, this is one of the primary gaps in the business side of medical education. You might get lucky with some faculty in residency or fellowship who go out of their way to teach you—maybe because they're interested in the topic, or see that you're curious, or because their bonus structure is tied to revenue. If that's not the case, you're responsible for educating yourself. For that matter, even if you did learn about it in one of your classes, you need to understand the real-world implications once you're in practice—including if you're an employee, since it can have an impact on your bonus structure.

Before we get started, let me be crystal clear: This isn't about gaming the system or doing anything remotely unethical or illegal; I am talking about getting paid properly for the amount of work you do. And that starts with **understanding the rules of engagement.**

Contracts 101: The Foundation of How You Get Paid

With contracts, there is strength in numbers when it comes to negotiating a deal with insurance companies. The smaller you are, the less overall value you deliver to the provider, and they use that to their advantage.

- As a solo practitioner with no partners, you have no leverage.

- If you are part of a small multispecialty group, you have some leverage.

- If you are part of a larger specialist group with a few dozen members, you have significant leverage.

- As an employee who is part of a large corporate organization, your employer has lots of leverage, with the benefit accruing to you downstream.

Say you've hung up your shingle as a solo practitioner, just you, your medical assistant, and no partners. Blue Cross, Medicare, Aetna, Cigna, and all the rest of them aren't just going to call you out of the blue and offer their insurance. When you call them, I hate to tell you, you're in a tough spot. They might offer 70% of Medicare, take it or leave it. (While you're thinking to yourself, "I already lose money on every Medicare patient. Now you want me to take 30% less?")

Perhaps you're a member of the Five Docs R Us LLC multispecialty group, with five members: a family doc, pain management doc, mental health counselor, dermatologist, and a nutritionist. You have more value now, so the carrier is willing to offer a better rate—but keep in mind, that's at the corporate level, not for you as the individual. The entity is applying for the contract.

One step above that is if you're part of a larger specialist organization, such as US Dermatology Partners or one of the state-based ortho organizations. When I was a member of a large ortho group in Arizona, we had a network of 60 or 70 orthopedic surgeons, which got us a seat at the bigger table. When we could prove to a big provider with metrics that we didn't do unnecessary surgery, for example, we were able to secure more than 100% of Medicare. Everything has a tradeoff, though: Because our group had its own overhead, we had to pay overhead to them to do the work.

The advantage of a larger entity like that is leverage, but you still need to do the math. Is it worth it for you to be under their umbrella, paying a certain amount of dollars each month in exchange for a better contract (with no negotiating needed on your part), while losing some autonomy and control?

A professional service agreement (PSA) offers a similar model to the group contract, in which you have an agreement with a large entity such as a hospital system, but you run your own private practice and you are considered an affiliate rather than an employee. You get the hospital contract rate, but they also take a cut when they do the billing. As with the previous example, this also comes with a slight loss of autonomy. They're going to want you to do a certain level of your surgeries or procedures at their facilities, not just at a location where you might have a partial ownership or other financial incentive.

When You're an Employee, Don't Assume It's Forever

Now, if you are an employee at a large hospital system or other healthcare entity, there's another nuance here—and it's vital to understand for your optionality. Yes, currently your employer has the contract at a corporate level. They're doing the billing and paying you X dollars a month, and you don't even think about it.

But this is important: What happens if you decide you want to open a private practice down the street, or to move to North Dakota to start one? What's your plan if you get fired or laid off, or your spouse secures a dream job on the other side of the country? All of a sudden, you need your own contract. It's not an impossible hurdle, but it's also not like flipping a switch. By the time you submit the paperwork and a carrier responds, the process can take three to six months; Medicare is the speediest at 30 days.

Unless you think you can charge cash while you wait—or you've saved enough money to not worry about paying the bills for a while—you need to have the foresight to plan out that move.

The solution: *If possible, always have your own contract through your MD PC or DO PC, even if you're not using it, and even if the rate isn't what you want.* This shouldn't be an afterthought, but rather part of your strategic plan that gives you future flexibility. You want to be able to call each carrier and say you'd like to activate the contract on XYZ date.

As discussed in the previous chapter, I'm a proponent of developing relationships with people in the insurance end of the business. The carriers know that physicians come and go, and you can lay the groundwork with them. You don't need to say you're planning on leaving your current employer or think you're about to get fired. It's better to say something like, "I'm considering an alternative strategy. What are the steps I need to take to get an individual insurance contract with you? Approximately what would the rate be?"

This also works in reverse. You're in private practice and have your own contracts already, but you've got a too-good-to-refuse offer to become an employee or join a larger entity that handles contracts and billing. After a certain time, the insurance carriers will consider your MD/DO PC contract to be inactive. Different carriers will have different timelines for that, but if it goes long enough, the contract becomes void and you need to reapply. Thinking about optionality as our core principle, you don't want that to happen, in case you decided to go back on your own and needed those contracts again. Checking in periodically with the carrier while you're an employee, and not actively using the contract, could save your hide when it becomes a necessity.

A quick word about Medicare: While this is the easiest and fastest of all the contracts to get, it's no surprise why a lot of family doctors and doctors in general are dropping it; the rates aren't great. They'll see Medicare patients on a cash-pay basis—but remember, you can't see them cash pay if you have a Medicare contract! Sign that, and you are legally obligated to see those patients and accept what Uncle Sam sees fit to pay you.

Obviously, if you're practicing adult medicine and the community is highly populated by a Medicare demographic, then you probably want a contract with them, because that's who the bulk of your patients are going to be using.

No Two Contracts Are Alike

The variables that go into a contract are incalculable. If a patient asks you and another specialist in your field what their out of pocket is going to be for a given procedure, the difference in the figure can be significant—even with same insurance company, let alone with a different one. This is particularly true if the other physician has an older contract, which indicates a high probability that the allowable reimbursement is higher.

But a huge caveat here: Neither of you is allowed to disclose what your contract is; in fact, doing so is illegal. (Trust me, the insurance company wouldn't want you calling to complain about why your pay is lower for the same procedure.) I won't get on my soapbox here, but this is why governmental agencies wanting price transparency is so problematic—at least beyond what an individual practitioner's cash price is.

The Fine Print: Know Your Codes

Reading an insurance contract isn't anyone's idea of a good time, and I'd be willing to bet that the number of physicians who actually do so is in the low single digits. But in addition to having a healthcare attorney and an experienced physician review your document before signing anything, you should read it and familiarize yourself with what it contains before you bill a single patient.

When it comes to billing, there are two codes that matter:

- The *diagnosis code*, a combination of letters and numbers used to classify and identify diseases, symptoms, and other health-related conditions. The most widely used system is the International Classification of Diseases (ICD), with the current version being ICD-10.

- The *Current Procedural Terminology (CPT) code*, a combination of numbers and letters used to describe what services or procedures you provided, whether medical, surgical, or diagnostic.

Between the two, you are communicating everything the insurance company needs to know to process a claim. If I see a patient named Sam Jones who's experiencing right shoulder pain, that's ICD-10 code M25.511. That's the easy part.

When it comes to the CPT code—the services that I provide and how I get paid—it's a bit more complex. I haven't seen Sam before, and I meet the criteria for a level-three new patient visit, CPT 99203, for which the allowable in my contract is $100. But the insurance company doesn't just generate a payment; a couple of things could happen:

- It turns out that Sam has a $10,000 deductible, and he's met $0 of it, so you need to collect from him. (Your back office should have found that out in advance, but for the sake of argument, they missed it.) That means Sam owes all $100.

- Sam has a $50 copay, so you collect that up front, and then wait for the insurer to pay you the other 50 bucks. That works when the deductible has been met, assuming that he doesn't have coinsurance.

So, here's one oddity of the CPT coding system, at least at the time this book was published. Generally speaking, all of the possible CPT codes appear in everyone's contract, regardless of specialty. (Would it be odd for a psychiatrist to file a CPT code for an ACL reconstruction? Sure, and I suspect it would raise some eyebrows at the insurance company. But it's probably in there.)

There are 10 different codes for office visits, including new patients and follow-ups. As the number gets higher, so does the pay, regardless of carrier—and the code numbers are national, so they're the same in Chicago as they are in Clovis, New Mexico.

As you might guess, you need to satisfy certain criteria in your notes to be able to justify a higher-level 99204 versus a 99203 for a new patient evaluation, for example. What I've seen over the years, however, are the following two scenarios:

- Physicians who are thorough and do a good job with their patients' exams and document enough for the level four (99204), but only bill a level three because they don't know the guidelines. They did the work and shortchanged themselves. Maybe it's only a $20 difference for each instance, but multiply that out times 10 patients a day times 300 days in a year: Under-coding was effectively costing them $60,000! (Obviously, the actual numbers would depend on your contract.)

- On the other end of the scale, I've seen physicians who always manage to bill the highest possible levels—and when you look at the notes, if their charts were ever audited, they'd be in trouble. There's no way they could justify what they were charging based on the actual work performed.

The point is, it's not enough to just know the code number; you need to understand what guidelines or other metrics are required. For my own practice, I created a cheat sheet that served as a quick reference on how many bullet points I had to satisfy for the history, the physical exam, assessment, and plan for each CPT code. As an orthopedic surgeon, it would be almost impossible for me to bill a level five, since nothing I did would involve multiple organ systems. In contrast, a primary care doc can often get to level fours and fives because they're asking patients about the endocrine system and cardiac system, listening to heart and lungs, palpating the abdomen, etc. That type of examination is more time consuming, which is why it's supposed to pay more.

If the Code Doesn't Fit

While CPT codes are well established, there are occasions when there isn't a good fit. In one of my early practice groups, my senior partner and I both performed hip arthroscopy surgeries, which did not have recognizable CPT codes. You could take your chances and bill under what's called an unlisted code, but it was unlikely to be covered.

This is where our state ortho group came into play. Being a member of that larger group, and having that seat at the table, we were able to negotiate with the carriers to recognize the hip arthroscopy codes. It wasn't easy, and it was a data-intensive process. We needed to show the efficacy, as well as putting in a monitoring system to ensure physicians were not overusing that type of surgery. The carriers wanted assurance that more conservative treatments were the front line—and that overall, whatever we did was saving them money while delivering the best outcomes. To underscore my earlier point about contracts, there is strength in numbers. A solo practitioner, even with a revolutionary and provably efficacious technique, would not be able to negotiate that kind of deal on their own.

Leveling the Playing Field (Sort of)

A final concept to have on your radar is the relative value unit, also called an RVU. Any given CPT code will also have an RVU associated with it. While contracts may vary widely, this is designed to make the payment system somewhat more equitable to physicians, regardless of reimbursement differences between insurance providers. As with all things government, it gets complicated, but here are the basics: Centers for Medicare & Medicaid Services (CMS)—which maintains the official Physician Fee Schedule (PFS) on which most contract pricing is based—also establishes RVU codes based on the service, practice expense, and malpractice expense. These RVUs are converted into PFS payment rates through the application of a fixed-dollar conversion factor, and there are also tweaks based on geographic area.

In the real world, this is how it works: You get an employment agreement with a healthcare entity or hospital that states "We're going to pay you $X per RVU." Now it doesn't matter whether a patient has Aetna, Blue Cross, United Health, or whatever, you're getting paid the same amount. One more important nuance: In addition to how you're getting paid, the RVU is also commonly used as a metric for bonus structures—so make sure to look for that in any employment or partnership contracts.

Do the Right Thing

Let me reiterate: *CPT codes are not about what you can get away with.* They're about knowing what you should be doing for a patient, documenting it, and getting paid for it. All of that falls within the insurance carrier's guidelines, not your personal opinion.

Finally, CPT codes also have implications in boosting your ancillary income, such as:

- Subcontracting to a physical therapist
- Durable medical equipment
- In-office lab work and X-rays

I'll talk in more detail about those in the next chapter, which is a lot more enjoyable than talking about contracts. It's about how you can design your roadmap to financial and personal freedom.

PRACTICE PEARL

Tap into the Power of "Thoughtful Consideration"

The same fellowship director who gave me the tip about setting expectations for post-op pain had a specific way of dictating his operative reports. He would say, "This pathology was found in the OR, and thoughtful consideration was given to doing A, but we did B for the following reasons," and then he'd list them.

I started incorporating those two words—*thoughtful consideration*—into my operative dictations right then and there, but I didn't realize the full power until a few years later when I ran into him at a reunion. "You might be the only fellow who picked up on that and actually uses it and told me about it," he said with a laugh. "But when things go south and you have to deal with attorneys or go to court, I guarantee those two words mean a lot to a jury. They understand that there is human judgment, and you've put it on the record. Even if you say in hindsight that path A might have been better, you've told them the nuances of your reasoning and why you chose what you did."

Chance favors the prepared mind.

—LOUIS PASTEUR

———————

CHAPTER 6

Ancillary Income

*Medical Add-Ons that Can Expand
Your Revenues Along with Your Mind*

I WAS ON RECENTLY ON A FLIGHT with a pain management colleague of mine, headed up to Alaska to do expert witness work that I do once a month. It's a long trip, which always leads to wide-ranging discussions—and eventually we landed on medicine.

At one point, he said, "You know, it wasn't what I thought it was going to be."

My response to him was, "In part, I agree." I think you can safely say that about any career you choose, regardless of what you do. How do you know what it's going to be like until you're actually in it? People can tell you—your father, your mother, your neighbor, your whoever—what it's like if they were in the same field, but it's always through their lens. That doesn't make it yours, and things change.

In high school, I had a paper route, back when that was still a thing. One of the customers in my neighborhood was an oral surgeon, and he kept telling me, "Don't be a doctor. It's not what it used to be."

And I'd think to myself, well, I don't know what that means. As a 16-year-old kid, I don't know what it is now, let alone what it used to be. I'd wanted to be a doctor as long as I could remember, maybe four years old, and as a high schooler, I felt like he was bursting my bubble.

At the heart of his comment, though, there's a kernel of truth. You pour a lot of blood, sweat, and tears getting into med school, which you assume is going to be a lot more work than undergrad. Then you get through med school, and you think, "Great, now I'm a doctor!" before arriving in residency (plus or minus fellowship) and realize there are new levels of pain and sleep deprivation you can achieve. Next, it's time to start your practice, which presents a new variant of stress and grinding, because now the buck stops with you. There's no longer an attending to bounce questions off of when you're unsure how to treat someone. You look behind you, there's nobody there. When you're in med school and residency you're learning the nuts and bolts. It's when you get into practice that the true learning begins.

I don't say this to discourage you about your choice of a medical career, the way that oral surgeon did to me way back when I was handing him that evening's copy of *The Pittsburgh Press*. But it is certainly a reality check. And this chapter, along with the next two, are geared toward giving you a mental and financial boost, whether you have concerns about your current or future income, larger aspirations on the business side of medicine, or simply want some projects that will keep you engaged at a higher level in your career.

Regardless of which or how many of those situations apply to you, throwing some supplemental income into the mix can mitigate them. The good news: You're simply adding on to elements of treating patients that you already are good at or know how to do.

Here are eight ways to start brainstorming your next move:

1. BILL SMARTER WITH AN IN-HOUSE PHYSICAL THERAPIST OR CERTIFIED ATHLETIC TRAINER

This is one of the occasions when knowing the CPT code can pay off with a little extra income to your bottom line. For example, the code for an initial patient evaluation is 97001. A patient presents with shoulder pain, and in your professional opinion, it's a minor impingement that can be adequately treated with physical therapy. You have two options: 1) Give them a script for PT and tell them to find one on their own or 2) Recommend a PT that you know and trust.

But what if you could refer them to a PT in your office or right down the hall? As long as you give the patient options, you're allowed to send them to your own PT. (Important: Medicare has a specific set of rules and regulations you must follow in every situation, and referring patients to your own PT clinic is among them.) In addition, a PT's contract with an insurance carrier will have lower reimbursement than a physician's in almost every case, making it potentially more lucrative for both of you if they bill under your contract.

I've had colleagues who took a similar approach with certified athletic trainers (ATCs), who happen to have pretty darn good knowledge of musculoskeletal medicine because they treat injured athletes all day at a high school or college. They know how to do exams, and many of them have worked in PT clinics, so they know the ropes in rehab. In one case, a physician I know used an ATC as a physician extender: They'd take a patient history, do an exam, and present to her just like a med student or a resident, and all she needed to do was double check the key findings. In cases where a patient didn't need an MRI, surgery, or even formal visits with a PT—and as long as they were self-motivated—the ATC would teach the patient some home exercises and maybe do a follow-up to make sure they stayed on track. The result? The patients were happy because

- It was convenient.
- They were working with somebody the doctor trusted.
- They didn't have to make multiple appointments to see a therapist.
- They saved on the copays.

Another variation on the theme: I've known other doctors who employed an ATC and sent them to a course to get certified as a first assist, which then allowed them to bill that code. The ATC is happy because you're probably paying them better than they would have been if they were just working for a high school. You're making some extra money because you're billing for the first assist component, and it's usually cheaper to hire an ATC than a PT. *Important! Different states have different rules, regulations, and policies about what an ATC can and can't do. If you are interested, I recommend investigating your state's current guidelines.*

Note that adding a PT or ATC to your lineup isn't restricted to orthopedics. Any field that has procedures involved might consider it as an avenue for improving patient satisfaction as well as a slight boost to the bottom line.

As a practical matter, it's slightly easier to have PTs or ATCs as W-2 employees working directly for you, partly because of regulations about billing and the need to access electronic medical records (EMRs). If you prefer to work with someone as an independent contractor, sending them a 1099-NEC at the end of the year, you will want to discuss that with your CPA or attorney to create the appropriate documents and agreements.

2. MAKE LAB WORK CONVENIENT FOR PATIENTS

This can be a suitable add-on for primary care, internists, family medicine docs—anyone who's regularly ordering lab work on their patients, whether it's lipid panels, thyroid function tests, or anything else. The upside to that is (you guessed it) because the CPT codes for lab work are already in your contract and you can make some extra bucks from doing something you're already doing: recommending Patient X get these labs done. But instead of sending them to an outside facility, you're doing the blood draw in your office and sending it yourself to the lab.

As with everything else in business, you need to do a cost-benefit analysis of the upsides and downsides, and figure out how the process is going to work. If you're running a full day of clinic, you're not going to be doing that yourself. Your PA or medical assistant can do that, as long as they're trained properly. For the patient, there is a huge tangible benefit: convenience. They get their blood drawn without having to make an appointment to go to a lab.

Note that, even if you're an employee, you can still think entrepreneurially. Blood draws are a moot point as an employee working inside a hospital. The lab's on the third floor and the patient can take the elevator, or the phlebotomist will come to your clinic from down the hall. But what if your employer asks you to staff a satellite clinic a few days a week that doesn't have convenient lab access? Put on your entrepreneurial hat for a moment. You could make an agreement with the hospital that you're going to have the blood draws done by your medical assistant on the days you're there. When you're at the hospital, it's business as usual; on the satellite office days, you're billing for the labs. Most physicians won't think to ask for an accommodation like that.

But look at it from the hospital's perspective: You're helping them grow their book of business.

3. IMPROVE YOUR IMAGE WITH IN-OFFICE X-RAY MACHINES

These are a common piece of equipment for a wide range of specialties, since the standard of care involves getting an X-ray. At the risk of climbing up on my soap box, I don't believe that's always necessary, but we've come to a place in society where that's the reality. I've seen insurance companies deny an MRI for a rotator cuff tear because X-rays weren't taken to rule out a fracture first. Somewhere along the line, the bean counters decided step one is to take a history, step two is an exam, and step three is "What does the X-ray show?"

If you're in musculoskeletal medicine, physical medicine, rehab/pain management, or family practice, or a host of other specialties, and you write a lot of scripts sending people to radiology facilities; it's inefficient. Yes, the patient can walk in to one of those facilities, but they're sitting there, waiting in line, wasting an hour or several, only to be told that they then need to see you again to score the results.

The downsides to having an in-office X-ray are obvious: The capital investment is high, followed by regular maintenance cost, plus labor because you need to employ a skilled X-ray technician. Moreover, you need to know the current guidelines for X-ray interpretation and billing as of whatever year you're doing this. Finally, they don't pay a ton per image, although an extra $20 here and $50 there adds up over time.

But consider the upsides:

- Convenience factor for the patient, not having to go to a separate location and sit in a waiting room.

- Real-time diagnostic value.

- A patient can't forget to get the images done, or to bring the images with them to their visit, and your office doesn't have to track them down to get them sent electronically. The opportunity cost of your staff's time spent on this is immeasurable.

Those upsides are precisely why our group of orthopedic surgeons, family medicine, and sports medicine docs chose to invest in an X-ray machine, but we also took it one step further. Within our building there were a range of musculo-skeletal providers that weren't affiliated with our group: spine surgeon, chiropractor, pain management, and a hand surgeon. One of my former business partners knew the owner of one of the big radiology companies in town and asked if he'd be interested in renting one of the small suites and putting in an X-ray machine for the other tenants. It was a win-win for everyone, doctors, patients, and the radiology company, which naturally became the provider of choice for MRIs. (We investigated it, but it wasn't cost-efficient for them or us to have an onsite MRI.)

4. STRAP UP YOUR BUSINESS WITH DURABLE MEDICAL EQUIPMENT

During the first part of my career, after I'd done an ACL reconstruction on a patient, I'd call up the brace vendor and they'd come in, drop off the brace, and leave. That's it. No exposure, no risk, no nothing. Not only did I do the surgery, but it was also incumbent upon me or the PA to fit it on the patient.

One day, I ran the numbers. Blue Cross's allowable for the brace—a simple piece of plastic—was more than 50% of what I got reimbursed for an ACL surgery. After subtracting the office overhead, I was actually making less than the brace vendor! It was especially painful taking into consideration that the patient had free visits during the global period for three months after surgery, and I had the liability hanging over my head for many years to come.

So, I did some research, and discovered that I could get those same braces wholesale for under $100. Not only that, lo and behold, the CPT code for that brace was right there in my contract. All I needed to do was procure a decent inventory and put my practice's logo on everything for a little extra marketing and advertising buzz.

In your mind's eye, imagine me showing up to surgery looking like a traveling salesman who dressed up in scrubs instead of suit and tie. The trunk of my Audi was packed with all sorts of stuff, from braces to ice machines. As I walked up to the surgery center, schlepping my medical bag, braces, and crutches, with stuff falling out of my arms, and struggling to get my ID badge out to open the door, I'll never forget the look on people's faces: "Um, aren't you the surgeon?" Or colleagues who asked, "What the heck are you doing?"

Meanwhile, my thought bubble was, "Never you mind. I may look like a fool, but I'm almost doubling my revenue for what I was already allowed to do."

The types of specialties that can prescribe medically necessary DME aren't limited to orthopedists juggling crutches and braces—it runs the gamut from pain management specialists to geriatricians. (Think about how many people have back pain!) For that matter, PAs and nurse practitioners in your office can dispense DME too. Note that, to dispense DME for Medicare patients, you need to have a separate Medicare DME license.

The other aspect to successfully launching a DME program, however, is understanding the insurance implications. I knew a physician earlier in my career who was losing a ton of money on bracing, because he thought his responsibility began with fitting it on the patient and ended with billing the code. He didn't think to view it through the same lens as an office visit or surgery, let alone how it impacted the patient. What are the patient's benefits and deductible? Do they have a copay? What's the allowable? Working backwards, you can figure out what makes the most sense. If the allowable on a brace is $615 and Jack has met $0 of his deductible, he has two options: Run it through his insurance and fork over $615, or cash pay on the side for $200.[6] You can't go wrong by doing right by your patient as well as your practice.

5. INVEST IN YOURSELF WITH DOCTOR-OWNED SURGICAL CENTERS

Standalone surgery centers often offer efficiencies and conveniences that you won't find at a hospital. All of the surgical fields—including orthopedics, plastics, neurosurgery, general surgery —often choose to do outpatient procedures at surgery centers, as do gastroenterologists doing endoscopies and colonoscopies. The same applies for family doctors who do sports medicine, given the right training and appropriate

---

6   This is a very simplified example—but reality is more complicated. There are three important steps to consider: 1. The patient is told "Your insurance covers this, but because your deductible is not met, your cost would be $X" or "Our cash price is $Y, and you may choose that instead, but it will not be submitted to insurance." 2. The patient signs an insurance opt-out/self-pay waiver and an acknowledgment that they are choosing self-pay, no claim will be submitted, and the self-pay price is final. 3. The provider confirms that the contract with the insurer does not require billing for covered services, and the discount is compliant.

privileges, dermatologists who perform skin procedures like Mohs surgery, or pain management physicians who do spinal injections.

The thought for consideration here is: What if you did procedures at a physician-owned surgery center where you had a stake in the business? Not only do you get paid the fee for the procedure, but part of the business profit from the facility fee paid by the patient and insurance carrier goes back to you. Depending on the arrangement, every month, quarter, six months, or annually, the leftover after overhead gets distributed to the physician owners. As part of a busy, well-run surgery center, you can make a fair amount of money doing that with no extra cutting, sewing, or scoping on your part.

I've participated in several such arrangements over time, and the easiest way to think of it is as an equity membership. Like a fancy country club, they don't just let anyone in—you need to prove your value. You typically have to show them that you have cases that you're going to bring there. Once you have privileges and do enough cases, at some point the board may take notice of the volume and revenue you've generated and offer you an invitation to join. The offering is typically a certain number of shares, with the price based on what the current valuation of the center is.

The next level up in complexity (and potential income) is to band together with a group of physicians and start your own surgery center, which is what I did in 2012. While it's possible to completely DIY the process, let's just say it's exceedingly complicated. Instead, we worked with a surgery center development company to put everything together and handle all the details. Yes, they took some equity, but it was well worth it for the ease and confidence in knowing it had been done correctly. My capital investment was $32,500, and there were months in which I earned several times that in a distribution. Adding to the phenomenal ROI, we eventually sold the center to a large surgery center ownership group that owns numerous surgical centers around the country, while retaining a minority ownership. (Stay tuned for chapter 9, when I'll share what I did with the capital gain.)

If you are considering an ownership stake in a surgical center, you will want to investigate and adhere to the present rules and regulations regarding disclosure to your patients about your ownership in that center.

6. MAKE MONEY ON THE ROAD WITH LOCUMS TENENS

I addressed this earlier as a possible practice model, and it's a little different from the add-on services above, but it still fits the definition of ancillary income from seeing patients. Not only are you paid a higher hourly rate, but everything is negotiable when it comes to locums as a side gig, down to whether you prefer a fixed per diem vs. reimbursement for expenses such as mileage, travel, meals, lodging, etc. Another benefit to locums work is the flexibility. Once you're on the radar of a hospital or locums staffing agency, usually from being licensed in their state, they'll reach out to you on an as-needed basis. You can dictate how much you want to work as far as a day-, week- or month-long assignment, plus you can skew your choices towards the locations you want to work in. Keep in mind, many if not most locums opportunities require independent contractor status, and state income tax laws vary widely. If you're doing work outside your state of residence, that's something you will want to discuss with your accountant long before tax time rolls around.

7. WORK FROM ANYWHERE WITH THIRD-PARTY TELEMEDICINE

Even though there weren't many positives that came out of the Covid pandemic, I'd argue one of them was the loosening of regulations on telemedicine. Working with your own patients via videoconference has become more common, and a lot of practitioners have added it as a side gig too. Doing telehealth for a third-party provider isn't necessarily a fit for all specialties, but it can be an option for any kind of primary care physician or pediatrician, and there's a particular need for mental health providers such as psychiatrists and clinical psychologists. It's a good way to provide care for underserved communities, so you can feel good about that too. You'll want to make sure that you have the appropriate licensing, and that you don't have any contractual conflicts if you work for an employer. Again, always consult with your CPA regarding income tax laws/rules in different states.

8. DISPENSING PHARMACEUTICALS AND OTC DRUGS OR PRODUCTS

The current world of pharmaceutical drugs in this country is crazy, and there's a whole host of reasons for that, from the enormous R&D spend by the pharma companies to pricing control by the Pharmacy Benefit Managers, a.k.a., PBMs. As physicians, we are technically allowed to dispense, with the caveat that you need to do your own research and talk to your attorney about what today's nuances are. The regulations vary considerably from state to state. At the basic level, it requires creating a separate entity and acquiring a pharmacy license through your state pharmacy board.

There is an alternative route, however. There are entities that provide these pharmacy services for you: You pick what meds you want, you pay them, they provide the meds and whatever kind of mini-safe is required, and then you bill out. While it may not be as profitable as forming your own entity, it's more streamlined and easier for you, since they know all the I's that need to be dotted and T's that need to be crossed.

Dispensing meds right out of your office can be a convenience for the patient as well as a contributor to your practice's bottom line. Urgent cares around the country commonly follow this model. As with every aspect of medicine, you absolutely must do so not only in a way that adheres to your state's rules and regulations, but in a manner that aligns with ethical practices.

Stand Out…Or Get Left Behind

A common through-line in several of these ancillary activities is that most physicians will not do some of them or all of them, and you can make your practice stand out. Conversely, if enough colleagues in your specialty are offering services A, B, or C and you're not—you're going to look like an outlier and a less-appealing option.

An important caveat: I've focused on the potential for additional income here, but liability should be a critical part of your analysis. I know that some celebrities believe there's no such thing as bad publicity. Well, that isn't true with physicians. If you conduct business in any way that could be considered marginally unethical, take a moment to think about what that discovery would look like in a newspaper article or in front of a jury.

The bottom line: Look at your insurance contracts and the codes that are in there. Consider what other ways you might be able to expand your practice. See if there's something that you enjoy doing that you could add as an ethical part of your practice.

In the next chapter, we'll expand that concept beyond seeing patients in your office or virtually.

94

THINK OUTSIDE THE BOX

I read a few years ago about a group of five radiologists that moved to Australia, where nighttime in the US is daytime there. From their own clinical experience, they recognized that one of the biggest needs in US hospitals is an attending radiologist's interpretation of X-rays, CT scans, and MRIs at night. They contracted themselves out to various hospitals across the US, reading films in what would be the middle of the night, when there might be a resident available but not an attending radiologist to provide the official read. Not only were they commanding a healthy sum for the service, but they also rotated so that each of them worked for one week and then took the next month off. It was a genius idea.

PRACTICE PEARL
Follow Up

I know phone calls aren't fashionable nowadays, but they remain among the best, time-tested ways of strengthening a patient relationship. If I operated on someone in the morning, I'd call them later that day to check in. "Hey, Joe, I know I talked to you in the recovery room, but you probably don't remember. Everything went well, I just wanted to make sure your knee's feeling okay." It's usually a 30-second phone call, but it shows you care—and it's effective marketing because they will tell that story to friends and neighbors. While I've used surgery as an example, it works in any field in which a patient had a concerning situation and following up will show them you care.

Like the phone, handwritten notes may be a dying art, but that makes them even more impactful. I created short template letters for new patients welcoming them to the practice, but here's the key: The salutation and signature areas were left blank. At the end of the clinic day, my medical assistant would print out the letters, and at the top I'd handwrite "Dear So-and-So," and at the bottom I'd write something personal. It could be something simple like "Great to meet you—let's see what the MRI shows," or "Hope the knee feels better so that you can do that hike into the Grand Canyon—looking forward to hearing about it." Then I signed my name and dropped a few business cards into the envelope. You'd be amazed how many people said, "I can't believe my doctor hand wrote a note." They didn't even care about all the general verbiage; it was my chicken scratch and the fact that I connected with them on a personal level.

CHAPTER 7

Alternatives to Treating Patients

Side Gigs that Leverage Your Medical Expertise

CALL IT A SIDE GIG, side hustle, moonlighting, or whatever you want. Your medical degree is your roadmap's perfect avenue into making more money without treating more patients—and with the potential of turning into something that offers work-life advantages too.

When I was telling a friend about my plans for this book and this particular topic, he made a comment that stuck with me. "You know what's extremely hard in medicine?" he said. "It's pivoting."[7]

You spend so much time and effort getting to the practice stage that the psychological notion of making a shift once you get there is extremely daunting. If you aren't focused 100% on patient care, what the heck was all that effort for?

At the risk of beating the same drum again: *As a doctor,*

---

7   This is a good place to recommend two websites that I consider exceptional when it comes to expanding your perspective. The first is Kevin MD (https:// kevinmd.com/) which assembles a wide variety of insights and real-world stories from physicians. The second is Doximity (https://www.doximity. com/), which is not only a forward-thinking communications platform for physicians, but also a great source for medical news and education.

you have the most marketable degree around. The issue is overcoming the psychological blocks to pivoting. It requires giving yourself a legitimate reason to adjust your course and being comfortable with making that commitment. I'm not saying you throw your diploma in the shredder and get business cards emblazoned with MEDICAL ENTREPRENEUR. This is about considering other paths that can coexist and aren't strictly focused on patient care. Maybe you continue treating patients while building up your side gigs for a few hours a week—simultaneously doing two things that you enjoy and find rewarding. I've also seen colleagues who ultimately realized medicine was not for them, and explored another avenue well enough that they made a lateral move into a new career altogether.

You can't know what's going to happen, and that's OK. It's no different from taking classes in college that weren't pre-med and exposing yourself to other ideas, people, and skill sets. If you don't experiment outside your comfort zone now, you're limiting your optionality in the future.

So, let's dive in on some of the alternatives you might want to consider.

EXPERT WITNESS WORK

I was brand new in practice and had never seen the inside of a courtroom, let alone had I any idea of what an expert witness was. My then-employer was out of the country and his office got a phone call from a workers comp adjuster asking if he was available. The assistant told them he wasn't available, but asked if they'd be willing to give his new associate—namely me—a try. I'm surprised the adjuster said yes, because I later learned that they don't usually randomly try out newbies, despite claims they want new blood in the industry.

In any case, the assistant asked me if I was interested, and I asked her what it entailed. "Basically, it's a second opinion for a workers comp claim," she said. "The person comes in for an independent medical exam (IME); you take a history and do a physical exam, but you don't tell them what you think. Then, you look at their records and write a report summarizing your findings, which includes answering some questions from the requesting party."

It sounded simple enough: It was what I was already doing, except someone else was coming up with the questions and I wasn't the person's doctor, and they weren't my patient.

I see the claimant, who had a legitimate multi-ligament tear in his knee. Among the questions is: "What is the impairment rating?" In workers comp, that's fancy medical terminology for determining just how worse off the person is due to the injury, and the adjuster uses that number as part of the calculation of a monetary payout. In this case, it was a pretty serious injury, and given that the knee is one of the more crucial joints in the body, I came up with a figure of 25% for the report.

The next day, the phone rings. It's the adjuster. "Doctor, did you mean to say 25% impairment rating?" In my head, I'm thinking maybe I did the numbers backwards, and they wanted the impairment in the form of 100% minus that number. "Oh," I said. "Was I interpreting this wrong? Should it have been 75%?"

I could hear her sigh on the other end of the line. "No," she said. "Did you use the book to come up with the number?"

My response was, "What book?" and that was pretty much the end of me doing IMEs at that time. It turns out there's basically a Kelley Blue Book of value for IMEs—the AMA

Guides to the Evaluation of Permanent Impairment[8]—only instead of pricing cars, it prices out values for injuries to the human body, in the form of percentages. Lesson learned, the hard way.

But life has a funny way of giving you second chances. A few years later, I was approached by someone who does marketing for an IME company, and she asked if I'd be interested in doing work for them.

This time, I was smart enough to get a copy of the book before diving in. Each chapter covers a different organ system/region of the body, be it arms, legs, spine and pelvis, the cardiovascular system, or pain. When I ran the numbers, I realized the guy I'd seen with the ligament tears would have had an impairment of 10% or 12%, not 25% and certainly not 75%. Next, I attended a conference held by the American Academy of Orthopedic Surgeons about workers comp and IMEs, and I felt like I was finally prepared.

I started doing IMEs once or twice a week while my main focus was still treating patients; but my skillset and expertise allowed me to grow that part of my business quickly.

By the time I moved away from clinical practice, I had connections throughout the entire system who would refer me for expert witness work—record reviews, IMEs, hearings, depositions, and trials—including IME companies, insurance adjusters, attorneys, and judges in a several states. How can

---

8   Although the AMA guide is technically the industry standard, there are significant nuances to how it gets used. There have been multiple editions published over the years; not only do different states use different editions, some require the use of their own supplemental guides too. Do your homework!

you succeed in this space, too?[9] For me, it comes down to the three A's: Availability, Affability, and Ability, in that order.

- Make yourself available. (If the adjuster needs an IME within three weeks, don't say your next availability is in three months!)

- Turn around reports in a timely manner and answer all the questions.

- Answer questions without waffling—speak clearly, make eye contact, and focus on educating the jury or judge. But be likeable... even if someone is trying to get under your skin.

- Be honest—your opinion can't be in your client's favor every time.

Note that performing IMEs doesn't necessarily require testifying in court. There were months where I did more than 100 evaluations, offering second opinions on workers comp and personal injury cases—without ever setting foot in a courtroom. I perfected a system to ensure that I was able to do as many as possible, without the quality suffering and without harming my regular practice.

One of the key benefits of doing IME work is that you're not treating these individuals, so your malpractice exposure is much less (though you still need to have malpractice insurance that covers you for IMEs). You're seeing them in the office, taking a history, doing an exam, looking at all the medical records, and writing a report that renders your

---

9   Note: IMEs are generally a realm most suited to specialties such as orthopedic surgery, pain management, spine surgery, and neurology, although there may be opportunities outside of those if you choose to pursue them.

opinion. Another benefit can be the ability to procure IME income through a different entity, separate from your medical practice one, which may allow you to have a different retirement plan (e.g., defined benefit plan). Talk to your CPA about what might be applicable in your individual circumstance.

A final note: If you are an employee, you should verify that your contract doesn't prohibit IME work and/or get permission as needed before pursuing this avenue.

CONSULTING

I'll break this concept into two different categories. First, general consulting could include advising physician groups, hospital systems, or even government agencies, helping them improve their business or organizational practices based on your medical knowledge and experience. I even have colleagues who extended that into advising on real estate, a topic which we'll address at greater length in the next chapter.

Second, you have consulting that you can do for pharma, biotech, and medical device companies. Over the years, I've consulted for a couple of different orthopedic medical device companies. In one case, they were a local startup that I contacted because I liked their product, but also had a slightly faster technique that achieved the same or better clinical results. I ended up doing product testing and teaching labs for them as a consultant, but I also saw three possible outcomes that influenced how I approached them for an agreement: They might fail, go public, or get acquired. Rather than getting paid hourly for consulting and getting a "sure thing" even if they didn't succeed, I thought it was worth a chance asking for equity. After all, I was indirectly going to be impacting their sales every time I taught a lab to a new batch of surgeons. They agreed to the deal.

Fast forward, and at some point, I was no longer using their implants or teaching for them. Then, one day, I get a check in the mail from Zimmer. The former startup company had been acquired and my stock had paid out. The reason I bring this up isn't to brag about my amazing foresight or good fortune, but rather to say: Assert yourself, because no one is going to voluntarily say, "Hey, Doc, would you like some stock options?" ***You don't get what you deserve; you get what you negotiate.***

HEALTH INSURANCE ADMINISTRATION

Most insurance companies don't have just a single medical director, there's usually a multitude of them at a state level or division level. While being a medical director can be a 9-5 job, there are some positions that are available on an ancillary basis. As an example, I had a colleague with a busy practice who served as a part-time medical director for an insurance carrier, primarily dealing with workers comp claims and overseeing the necessity of different surgical procedures.

ADVISORY BOARDS

I've served on several advisory boards for startup companies, and for several years I've been part of an angel investing group, Arizona Tech Investors. Whenever there's a startup pitch that's medical in nature, I have more value to add than a colleague who is, say, a real estate investor or software CEO. As with the consulting example, there's negotiation involved and your position as a physician can provide leverage. If I like a company enough to invest, I recognize that I may lose it all. But if I request some equity shares to serve on their advisory board, I'll be doing everything I can for them to succeed—they're not just getting my money, they're getting my connections.

SPEAKING AT CONFERENCES

Many speaking gigs are for exposure, or offer a small honorarium that barely covers your hotel night. But there are a few niches like pharma companies, where a primary care doc, dermatologist, or pain management physician might make sense as a paid spokesperson, including compensation plus flights, meals, etc., to speak to a given group. Obviously, this won't just magically happen. If you've seen good results with your patients, ask the sales rep if there might be some opportunities to expand your relationship with the company.

TEACHING

This is distinct from going into academic medicine. I've taught lectures on insurance coding as well as surgical procedures at a local university, and while it wasn't lucrative, it was rewarding because I was helping guide the next generation of medical practitioners. The good news is that this is one of those areas where your MD or DO eliminates a barrier to entry—you don't have to have a master's degree in education to be adjunct faculty. There are side benefits to it too: If you're teaching a class, you'll add to your network; students may follow you on social media (if you have a presence) and you may get some patients out of it in a roundabout way. Beyond that, adding adjunct faculty at a medical school to your CV builds your credentials for job searches, and it gives you credibility if you're testifying in a legal proceeding.

INVENTING

Have an idea for an implant or something that could be an innovative tool in the OR? Or maybe a device or app that can enhance patient care in general and improve patient satisfaction? Draw it on a napkin and contact a patent attorney to learn about protecting your intellectual property (IP). From there, you can take a couple of routes, either talking to a mechanical engineer or software engineer, etc., who can make it and test it, or reaching out to a medical device company. (Make sure they sign non-disclosure agreements.) If a device company builds and sells it, you'll get royalties (if you make sure your agreement specifies this). While this may sound like a lottery ticket, stranger things have happened—and you don't want to be the person who has an idea and then says, "Yeah, but what do I know? How am I going to do this?" Think of the Debakey forceps found in every OR, or the more recent example of Proactiv, skin-care products developed by dermatologists Katie Rodan and Kathy A. Fields. Inventions don't need to be limited to medical ideas, either—it can include tailoring a broad category of services to doctors using your knowledge of the nuances. For example, Doc2Doc Lending (doc2doclending.com) is a financial products and services company focused solely on medical professionals. Bottom line: Be creative.

FILE REVIEWS

Many organizations need board-certified physicians to do file reviews, also known as chart or medical record reviews, as objective third parties. This category is different from the expert witness work described above, and it also can be technically done by physicians from any specialty. You're not seeing a patient directly—and again, it is not a patient-doctor relationship, but you are rather examining their records to make a determination about their care. In addition to being well compensated, these gigs have the benefit of being a home office or remote work that you can do just about anywhere. SEAK (nonclinicalcareers.com) conferences are a great way to connect with companies that need these services. Keep in mind that you should check with your malpractice insurance carrier whether you are covered for this type of activity under that policy or if you will need to procure a separate policy.

One other item to keep in mind: When I was practicing, I found myself on the wrong end of reviewers on multiple occasions, receiving denials of a procedure that I was confident would be efficacious. In one case, a denial letter was authored by a cardiac surgeon who probably didn't know much about shoulder surgery. I suspect a lot of physicians might just tell the patient they were denied, because they don't want to waste their time calling the carrier. But just as I know that a heart surgeon would be annoyed if an ortho denied a heart bypass, I wasn't going to let this go. I set up a peer-to-peer call with another reviewer who was an orthopedist, and this time the procedure was approved. While you don't have to be in the specialty that a file review is in, you should also recognize when you're out of your lane. And as a physician in your own practice, you should fight for your patient's interests.

LIFE CARE PLANNING

This is a subcategory that technically falls under the expert witness umbrella—with similarities to file reviews too—but warrants a separate mention. In brief, this is about creating comprehensive long-term plans in personal injury and elder law cases, usually dealing with situations such as catastrophic injury or chronic illness. Until I got involved doing expert witness work, I'd always assumed it was nurses who created these plans, but it turns out physicians are often desired due to the additional level of credibility we bring to the process.

Unlike expert witness work, however, you're not acting as an expert testifying in court. They send you a file with guidelines to create a plan for a plaintiff, which could include how many doctor visits they'll need per year, and what types of medications, physical therapy, home health care, etc. Besides the fact that you can do this at home or remotely, another nice aspect of this is that you don't have to have an active clinical practice.

PAID MEDICAL SURVEYS

There are dozens if not hundreds of organizations that will pay you to take qualitative or quantitative surveys, including SERMO, M3 Global Research, and a variety of others. (From personal experience, I can tell you I receive at least five emails a week offering to pay for my thoughts via a medical survey.) Depending on your specialty, topics might include product feedback, emerging therapies, drugs, or interventions, and clinical observations. These won't replace the income from your day-to-day practice, but it comes down to calculating how much your time is worth. Is there a better way to spend 30 minutes than answering questions? Is it something you could do on the phone during a half-hour commute, instead of listening to music or talk radio? It also depends on where you are in your career—as a resident, $100 might be the difference between staying at home vs. a night out on the town.

CREATIVE PURSUITS

When I attended a SEAK conference a few years ago, one of the session speakers said something that has stuck with me: "Good things happen to physicians who write." That applies to anything from authoring an IME report to writing a book. (Hey, that's what I'm doing right now!) For some doctors, like

Michael Crichton and Robin Cook, their fame as novelists and within Hollywood far exceeds anything they're remembered for in medicine.

If you're somebody who enjoys writing for fun or stress relief, who's to say that isn't a possible path? Even if you don't have the skills or time to write a screenplay or book, keep in mind that TV and movies have a significant demand for medical knowledge. Heck, even the TV show *Friends* had an episode in which Ross had a mysterious skin growth on his butt cheek. Now, am I saying that that required medical knowledge? Perhaps not, but the point is that medical content is everywhere, and I want you to start noticing it now that I've put that thought into your brain.

Make no mistake, there are huge hurdles to breaking into showbiz, but it's not impossible. Ken Jeong, whose acting credits include *The Hangover* movie series and the TV sitcom *Community*, took theater classes as an undergrad at Duke, performed at local comedy clubs while in med school at UNC School of Medicine, and won the Big Easy Laff-Off during his residency at Ochsner Medical Center in New Orleans. He did double duty as a practicing internal medicine physician and stand-up comedian in Los Angeles before committing to full-time Hollywood fame in 2006.

The common throughline in this pursuit, or anything else in this chapter, comes down to Newtonian physics: ***Inertia is hard to overcome and momentum is hard to slow down.*** Once you start it, the wheel starts moving faster.

SOCIAL MEDIA

This is an extensive enough topic that it requires research beyond this book and sweat equity on your own to make it work. Depending on your specialty and practice, social media can be a powerful way to market to and educate patients, and even to form stronger relationships. Turning it into a revenue source—beyond attracting new patients—is an entirely different level of commitment and requires an extraordinary number of followers. That said, it's not impossible. And one piece of advice: If you're part of a large medical group or hospital system, explore leveraging that system to engage a larger audience—while formalizing that any revenues generated are outside your employment agreement.

Four excellent examples of physicians who have created passionate Instagram followings:

- Dr. Sandra Lee @drpimplepopper
- Dr. Shereene Idriss @shereenidriss
- Dr. Joyce Park @teawithmd
- Dr. Muneeb Shah @doctorly

Managing Your Time and Expectations

Before we close out the chapter, a quick cautionary note to pace yourself. All the items above take time and effort, and if you want your clinical practice to thrive—let alone your personal relationships—you can't go chasing every squirrel. Ultimately it comes down to time management and what you're willing to commit to.

- Define your goals, as far as hours-per-month commitment and financial benefits of a given side gig.
- Measure your progress—and be honest with yourself.

- If you're getting solid return on investment, great!

- Some things won't pencil out, but there's no need to feel like you failed. Like they say in the mob movies, "It's just business."

- And some opportunities pan out at their own time—so never discard an idea; just leave it on the back burner as you may be able to resurrect it later.

An additional revenue stream comes in handy, whether you use the extra money to pay your student loans or mortgage, buy a new car, take a vacation, or sock it away in your retirement account for long-term financial freedom. Not only can it offer you financial peace of mind, it can also accrue to a better work-life balance and expand your overall network. If you succeed in one of these paths, you could cut back on your clinical work. Instead of seeing 40 patients a day, you see 20 and give them the time they deserve. Best of all, you're establishing a space in your brain that's not specifically about your day job—tapping into creativity that treating patients may not always offer.

WHAT ARE THE BENEFITS OF SIDE GIGS?

Here's what physicians responding to a recent Sermo survey[10] had to say:

41%	Earning extra income
21%	Improving their skills
17%	Having opportunities to expand their professional network

---

10 Sermo, "5 Best Physician Side Gigs to Make Passive Income," https://www.sermo.com/resources/side-hustle-for-doctors/

But there's another option to consider that I believe physicians are uniquely positioned to take advantage of, and we'll get to that in the next chapter.

STAYING ON THE GOOD SIDE OF THE IRS

If you haven't done contract work before, you need to realize that it's a different beast from being a W-2 or even operating a private practice. Your CPA or business advisor can provide customized advice on your situation, but here are some of the basics to have in mind:

- As of 2026, anyone who paid you more than $2,000 in the previous year will issue you a form 1099-NEC (non-employee compensation), and that figure will be indexed to inflation in 2027 and beyond. Regardless of the amount, no taxes have been taken out of that money, so Uncle Sam will want to see his share of your self-employment income on April 15.

- Important! If someone pays you less than the 1099-NEC threshold for a given year, or if they don't send you a 1099-NEC, that doesn't let you off the hook. You still owe taxes on that income.

- There can be tax advantages of 1099 income, including the ability to write off eligible expenses and your home office, but you need to make sure you are within the rules and regulations.

- For accounting and liability purposes—i.e., separating a side business from your other business interests—look into creating an LLC or other entity, acquiring a separate employer identification number (EIN), and opening dedicated bank and credit card accounts.

- We'll get into further details on this in chapter 9, but self-employment income can also offer advantages in investing, such as creating a solo 401(k) specific to this entity in addition to your other retirement vehicles.

A PLAY-BY-PLAY: PHYSICIAN VS. ATTORNEY

I recognize that some physicians may shy away from expert witness work because they don't want to deal with attorneys, and I won't sugarcoat it: You need to have thick skin. Lawyers can be nasty and badgering and take positions that have nothing to do with science or best medical practices. But at the same time, if they're attacking you personally, it's probably because their case is weak or flawed.

That's the negative side of it. I will submit, though, that this gives you an opportunity to prove that you're smarter than the average lawyer. A case in point: I'd been retained by the defense on a personal injury case in Alaska, in which a woman was suing her brother-in-law for bumping her leg with his car. Her claim was that she'd been badly injured, needing multiple surgeries. The counterevidence was that she was a large woman with pre-existing arthritis, and that the collision was at about 2 mph, and the only injury appeared to be a low-grade contusion.

I spent more than three hours on the stand, testifying about my IME report. The plaintiff's attorney asked all sorts of nonsense questions and accused me of relying on the affidavit of a treating physician who had done her knee replacement—but as it turned out, my IME report was dated four months before the other doctor's affidavit. "It appears," I said, "that the other doctor agrees with me, not the other way around." Score one for Team Physician.

Next, he displayed a classic example of how lawyers will attack you in a no-win way about your fees.

Let's say you charge $X and their expert charges $Y. If Y is less than X, they will position you as someone who overcharges. If Y is greater than X, they'll try to say their expert is more thorough and skilled. That's what this lawyer did: putting up a chart with a line-by-line comparison with his expert. Their expert was a few thousand bucks more, so out came the argument that he was more thorough.

"What do you have to say to that doctor?" the lawyer asked.

I looked at him and smiled, then turned directly to the jury. "Look, to be fair, I don't know Dr. Smith's reading speed or comprehension, so I can't comment on how long it took him to do this work," I said. "All I can tell you is that I was honest with my billing time." I didn't say the other expert wasn't honest; I merely wanted to plant the seed with the jury that I was. Score two for Team Physician.

Next, he went on an extended line of obscure tangents about affidavits and notaries, trying to make it look like I'd made a mistake in how I'd assessed the original doctor's affidavit. "Doctor, do you know this doctor? No? Were you there when he signed this affidavit? No? Is it notarized? No? Well, then how do you know he signed it?"

In my head, I made a decision: "Before I'm off this stand, I'm going to make you look like a schmuck."

Soon thereafter, he posted on the main court-room screen what he stated were cross-section MRI images of his client's spine. "Doctor, you would agree that these show my client's disc herniations?" he asked.

I looked at the images and smiled, because I

noticed something he hadn't. Again, I looked at the jury. "Well, I would agree that these images show disc herniations," I said. "But I cannot agree or state within a reasonable degree of medical probability that these show *your client's* disc herniations."

I could see the steam coming out of his ears. "What do you mean? How can you say that these show disc herniations, but you don't think they're hers?"

"To be fair, I don't know who put these images together," I said. "I wasn't there when they were done. They're not signed, there's no name on them, and they're not notarized. If something isn't notarized, how would I know exactly?" Score three for Team Physician.

The jurors were smiling or chuckling, which they're not supposed to do, and the defense attorney leaned back in his chair with a big smile on his face. He knew the case was won, and all that was left was formalities.

My point in telling this story is that, as much as we as physicians may fear the legal system and attorneys because of what's ingrained in our head about the malpractice world, it sometimes offers you a chance to dispense your own brand of justice, physician-style.

PRACTICE PEARL
Encourage Referrals

To me, word-of-mouth delivers the best ROI in the marketing world. It also indicates you're focusing on just doing a great job, and the marketing takes care of itself. Good patients tend to refer other good patients, because they know a referral reflects on them too—so they're unlikely to send you someone who's difficult.

I used to ask all my new patients "Who sent you to me?" (Nowadays, many of the online intake forms do this for you.) After the office visit, I'd either text the referring patient or send them a quick handwritten note to say thank you. In addition, I'd add them to a list, and the fifth time they referred a family member or friend, I'd mail them another thank you with a gift card for coffee.

CHAPTER 8

Real Estate Strategy

The Land of Opportunity...
and Additional Income

WHY ARE PHYSICIANS such a natural match for real estate investing? Part of the answer is disposable income. It takes money to make money, and that gives you an advantage for making high-dollar purchases. But it also comes with some synergies, since we are often office-based practices in high-traffic locations, which extends to specialized property types such as surgery centers or other outpatient facilities too.

There are several reasons that real estate is particularly attractive for doctors:

- Returns that (when structured properly) can often be higher than other investment vehicles, since you're getting a blend of cashflow and appreciation.

- Consistent, predictable income.

- Tax advantages.

- Portfolio diversification beyond the stock and bond markets and other assets.

- Hedging against inflation.

- Control over your destiny, if you're an owner-operator of a property that includes your practice.
- Building long-term wealth for your family.

Real estate investing requires an understanding of your risk tolerance and appetite for a little extra work, depending on how involved you want to be. Do you want to manage a property yourself, or should you hire a property manager to do it, knowing that will cut into your profitability? Everything has a tradeoff. You need a strategy.

Real estate investing also comes with a few caveats, especially the fact that property is illiquid. It can be tempting to get yourself overextended, and maybe you're OK for a while. When markets get tough, however, as we've experienced several times in the past two decades, you don't want to put yourself in a position without the liquidity to wait out the downturn.

As a result, it's yet another example of a situation in which you'll want to enlist the assistance of experts, such as a CPA, financial advisor, and lawyer. In addition, there are real estate brokers specializing in medical properties who can make your path much smoother if you decide to explore your options. Consider this chapter a basic starting point for your exploration.

Getting Started

In the real estate world, you'll hear the phrase "passive income." By the IRS definition, that means earnings from rental properties in which the taxpayer does not "materially participate." But that can be a bit misleading, if you're new to real estate: Even if you're heavily involved in managing a property, the default assumption is that rental activity is passive, which has tax implications that are beyond the scope of this book. (Have I mentioned you should talk to your CPA?)

First, let's discuss investing in real estate in a few places where it intersects with medical practices.

Most physicians in private practice will rent their space. Yes, they can write off the lease payments as a business expense, but they're not getting anything out of it beyond a place to practice. Inevitably, some will decide that owning a property is a better option.

But it's not as simple as buying a property under your own name. You need to create a separate LLC that buys the space, and your MD/DO PC pays rent to the LLC. Because it's a commercial property, you get depreciation—an accounting term for a gradual reduction in the value of an asset over time, which gives you an income tax deduction on the rental income you paid your LLC. A simple illustration: Instead of renting for $2,500 a month and deducting it as a business expense, you pay that $2,500 a month to the LLC, which pays the mortgage, property taxes, etc. Your net income after everything might be $1,400—which is way better than the $0 you get from renting, plus you own an asset.

You could stop right there, but the next level of sophistication is to buy a property with several offices—because a majority of physicians are probably going to rent. Your LLC is now renting to two other physicians, and you have another passive income stream. Plus, you're essentially paying rent to yourself through another entity.

Let's ratchet things up another notch. You're part of the Five Docs R Us multispecialty group. Between the five of you, you have enough resources to purchase an entire complex with even more space, under another LLC that includes all of you. You're all renting from that LLC, and you're able to rent to other people, with income accruing to the partnership.[11]

But pump the brakes for a second. The downside is you are now no longer just a landlord with a tenant or two; you have to deal with those four other people on a business level. Physicians change groups, and egos can get in the way. When relationships go sour, and they frequently will, you need to have agreements in place to decide how you will part ways amicably. Enlisting a healthcare attorney to create contract verbiage and a partnership agreement is paramount.

The other reason for making sure you have solid agreements is that you've now created an entity that might be appealing to an even larger entity, especially if it includes multiple specialties. In other words, you need to have an exit strategy for this possibility. There are a variety of ways this is commonly negotiated: For example, the large entity acquires the practices and you become employees, while your partnership continues to hold the real estate and let the healthcare organization pay you rent. If the multiplier is big enough, maybe you want to sell everything, lock, stock, and barrel.

Options Beyond the Medical Realm

Of course, many physicians expand beyond the bounds of medical buildings. Common real estate investing approaches include single-family homes, multifamily properties,

---

11   Whether you invest in two suites or an entire complex, think about it from a strategic perspective. It's beneficial to be selective about who you're renting to. Tenants can also be a referral source, whether they are physicians in different specialties that can drive business to your practice or they have the interest, money, and wherewithal to be co-investors in a PT clinic, for example.

non-medical office spaces, and retail or industrial properties. All of them offer opportunities if you're willing to do the research and fund the venture. I even know a former physician who has created a mini empire that includes entertainment venues and a microbrewery. If that sounds outside your comfort zone, there are a few other ways to engage in real estate investing to consider that don't require putting on your landlord hat.

SYNDICATIONS/CROWDFUNDING

Passive real estate syndications and crowdfunding are a way of pooling funds with other investors to acquire properties. Both strategies provide exposure to real estate and diversification, while the day-to-day details are handled by professional property managers.

REAL ESTATE INVESTMENT TRUSTS

This is the most hands-off way of diversifying into real estate. REITs trade like stocks, giving you exposure to real estate (including medical-specific) with more liquidity and without the physical management.

OPPORTUNITY ZONES

By any measure, Scottsdale, Arizona, is a pretty darn nice place: home to tens of thousands of millionaires, dozens of world-class resorts, and ranked in the top five cities by income in the US. So, it was a little surprising when I was in my car, about to hop on the highway, and saw a sign designated for an Opportunity Zone—a distressed area with special government incentives for private investors. The way they work is a bit complicated, but you're not buying a building, you're getting a fraction of a building that is managed by someone else and receive quarterly updates. This has financial implications, and some important benefits, that I'll discuss in the next chapter.

As noted above, you need to take a serious look at your risk tolerance before dipping your toes into real estate. This includes your spouse or significant other. As the landlord of a rental home, you need to be prepared for 3 a.m. phone calls that a pipe has burst or the air conditioner has died. But if you have extra money that you don't need for your living expenses, and you've already maximized your other options such as 401(k) and other retirement or investment plans, it can be an asset class that holds value over the long haul.

Unlike the complicated arrangements with my partnerships in medical buildings and surgery centers, I like to keep things simple with residential properties. I prefer long-term rental deals and using a property manager—it's like being on autopilot. The money deposits in my account every month, and really the only thing I have to do every year is to sign a new rental agreement.

Another tip, courtesy of my financial advisor, is to leverage your existing assets. I was in the process of purchasing a home for my parents in Los Angeles, right after the seller had a bidding war in which all the offers fell through. I used a line of credit through my financial account at a low interest rate to pay cash—a much more appealing offer to a skittish seller. Then, within 30 days, I secured a regular home loan and refunded my account.

Note: This isn't offered as specific financial or real estate investing advice, since every circumstance is different—only to remind you that you probably have more options than you realize!

As with medical properties, you need to begin with the end in mind. Why do I want to do this? What are my primary and secondary objectives? Am I satisfying those criteria? What are definite and potential downsides? If I move to Denver, am I willing to continue operating a property in Dallas from a distance?

THE ANATOMY OF A RENTAL OPPORTUNITY

Let's talk through a possible hybrid scenario—we'll call it "medical property adjacent." You're starting a residency in Ann Arbor, Michigan, but you've never lived there before and don't know the town. You rent for a year to get the lay of the land, and the potential is obvious. Ann Arbor not only has proximity to an international airport, but also University of Michigan, University of Michigan Medical School, and multiple large hospitals. In other words, between students, residents, and hospital and university employees, there's always going to be a market for rentals, with a good percentage of the tenants being transient.

One possible approach would be to buy a place, and live in it while you're a resident, with roommates if it's big enough. If you decide to stay in Michigan to practice, you're all set. If not, maybe you hold on to the place and rent it out to the never-ending stream of grad students and residents, earning passive income while building your equity in a desirable area. The residency graduate medical education office can offer great exposure, since they have listings of apartments and condos, and maybe you earn a reputation as the perfect place for doctors in a particular department or specialty. The point is, a rental strategy near a medical school complex doesn't require a 5,000-square-foot home—in fact, it probably shouldn't be, because what resident can afford that? Keep in mind, there's a difference between being a landlord for undergrads vs. med students and residents. Who's going to be more likely to have keg parties and trash the place? Probably not the latter two!

PRACTICE PEARL
Embrace "Yes… and…"

Speaking in public, including less formal settings like talking to colleagues and patients, is an essential skill for physicians. That may explain why my favorite class in college wasn't a pre-med prerequisite or a science class, yet it turned out to be incredibly useful.

We needed to take six credits in the theater arts, and my thought was "How hard could it be? I just aced organic chemistry." The first class I signed up for was Film Studies—which turned out to be more difficult than I imagined, even though we were basically watching and analyzing movies. Weirdly enough, the second class—the Art of Improv—changed my view of human interaction.

In improvisational theater, there's a principle known as "Yes… and…" Basically, you're trying to expand on concepts rather than squash them. You agree to something, no matter how ridiculous, and try to take it to the next level. Talented comedians on TV shows like *Whose Line Is It Anyway?* make it look easy. It's not. In improv, you need to think on your feet at every given moment. That's not easy, and when you're doing it in front of strangers, it's particularly daunting.

By some stroke of good fortune, one of my graduate student teaching assistants was Keegan-Michael Key, who was hilarious, and it doesn't surprise me he's gone on to an incredible career in movies and TV. But as talented as he was, there was nothing that he could do to save us from the final exam: Standing in front of 300 students staring at you in a large lecture hall, trying to make some random student smile within 60 seconds without using any words.

Now, I've never had a problem with public speaking, and I can probably credit my dad for that. He knows hard work, how to talk to people, and how to stick up for himself. But as those 60 seconds ticked down, recognizing this is not a buddy who I could make laugh in an instant, I realized this is different. It's the art of critical thinking. It's the art of not obsessing about what somebody else is going to think or say about you.

That's a mentality that I've carried forward, and I encourage you to too. If you can take an improv class, even better.

Inertia is hard to overcome, and momentum is hard to slow down.

—DR. AMIT SAHASRABUDHE

CHAPTER 9

Managing Your Money

How to Protect and Grow Your Wealth

I'VE SEEN IT HAPPEN. A smart, driven kid goes through all the stages, from being unsure if they're cut out for medicine to graduating with honors and becoming a superstar in residency. And then the first real paycheck lands in their account as an attending physician. "I've arrived!" Next thing you know, they've got a giant home with a Range Rover in the driveway and a boat on a trailer in the side yard. The physician trifecta is real, even if it's a cliché.

You have to ask yourself: Did I *need* all that stuff, or did I *want* all that stuff? Because there's a big difference. Nobody is saying that you can't or shouldn't do any of that if you can afford it. At the same time, understand that when you're first getting started, everything may seem rosy—but you don't yet know how the dominoes are going to fall. Remember, too: High income also means high taxes, so don't spend all your cash and be shocked come April 15 that you owe the IRS a hefty sum. Plan for that payment ahead of time.

Some experts will tell you to have three months of living expenses socked away, while others will say six months or two years. Figure out what might be best suited for you, but it should be there in case the you-know-what hits the fan.

If your practice starts to struggle, can you go 18 months without being paid? Maybe if you're 55 and you've put aside enough money, invested wisely, and don't lavishly spend on things, you might be OK. You can still pay the mortgage, or it's already paid off, the kids have already graduated college, you can put food on the table and so on.

But if you're in your early 30s, swamped with med school and credit-card debt, and now all of a sudden, you've got multiple payments on the best things in life? That's a brutal situation to be in, it's all too common, and it can totally veer you off your roadmap.

Sorry to Say, Money IS an Object

There's a general perception that money is no object for physicians. As you climb the economic ladder in your career, of course you can afford multiple homes, fractional jet ownership, and a yacht that's three feet bigger than your buddy's! But the cold, hard truth is that too many physicians are rich in paycheck but poor with their financial and business decisions. I'm not sure why that is, but my instinct is that it's because we delay economic gratification for a long time—and then when we finally start making good money, we're trying to make up for lost time.

To this point, I've talked a lot about the different ways to provide yourself career optionality and make more money. Let's switch gears a bit and discuss creating a strategy to protect what you've earned and grow it.

This chapter isn't going to be about specific stock recommendations or financial strategies. I'll leave that to market pundits and the various wolves of Wall Street. Instead, I'll provide a broader overview of some of the types of financial jargon and instruments you may not have encountered before. And this all comes with the disclaimer that I'm neither a CPA nor a financial advisor, but you can check out some of their wisdom in the two bonus chapters that follow this one. I recommend that you reach out to trusted experts in this field on your own.

The Rundown: The Basic Landscape of Retirement and Investing Plans

ACCOUNT TYPE	HOW IT WORKS/WHAT TO BE AWARE OF
Traditional IRA	Contributions are pre-tax; growth is tax-free; taxes paid when funds are withdrawn in retirement; income limit on being tax-deductible
Roth IRA	Contributions not tax-deductible, but you get tax-free growth and withdrawals; contributions limited by income
Backdoor Roth IRA	For high-income earners who can't contribute to a Roth IRA; nondeductible traditional IRA contribution plus traditional-to-Roth IRA conversion
Traditional 401(k)	Pre-tax employer program, with taxes when funds are withdrawn; is there an employer match?
Roth 401(k)	Hybrid employer program; contributions in after-tax dollars, then tax-free withdrawals
Solo 401(k)	Program designed for self-employment/1099 income with no employees (except spouse), with pre-tax or Roth 401(k) options; higher contribution limits than employer-based plans—can contribute as employee and employer profit share
Mega Roth 401(k)	Allows high-income earners to contribute extra money into a Roth account; after-tax contributions to a 401(k), converted into a Roth account for tax-free growth
Defined Benefit Plan	Also known as a pension plan; guarantees a specific, predetermined monthly income to employees during retirement
Profit sharing	Highly dependent on employer; important to know contractual calculations such as your share of overhead

Opportunity Zone Fund	Private investment vehicle that can defer capital gains taxes by investing in economically distressed areas; new rules with the new tax law start in 2027
Health Savings Account (HSA)	Tax deduction on contributions; can be used for health expenses, but also a good long-term savings vehicle similar to Roth: no tax on withdrawal or capital gains for qualifying health expenses
529 Plan	Tax-advantaged savings account for education expenses; can be for beneficiaries or self-directed; tax-free growth, and withdrawals are tax-free for qualified education expenses
Self-directed IRA/Roth IRA	Retirement account that allows investing in a wide range of alternative assets, including real estate, private companies, precious metals, or cryptocurrency
Whole/Universal Life Insurance	Premiums go towards death benefit and cash value; loans can be taken against cash value tax-free; withdrawals decrease death benefit

In addition to the regular contributions, many of those accounts (such as the various 401(k) and Roth IRAs) allow you to make so-called catch-up contributions when you are over 50. Starting in 2026, workers ages 60 to 63 can make even higher "super catch-up" contributions.

I won't go into minute details about each of those vehicles, because it would require an entire book to cover them all. I will, however, make some notes about a few of the tools that can be helpful for physicians in their financial planning and making their money go farther.

No one relishes the idea of being in a higher tax bracket, but it often means you have discretionary income. If you have discretionary income, then you're likely to be someone who can max out your IRAs and 401(k). . . and then still do something else with the rest. Here are a few of my favorite lesser-known vehicles for maximizing wealth:

OPPORTUNITY ZONES

One of my biggest financial successes was when I sold my majority stake in the surgery center that I helped start. The return on investment was phenomenal. We negotiated the sale of our center to a large surgery center group that owns a lot of surgery centers around the country, while keeping a minority ownership. I received a nice check, and could have paid the capital gains and enjoyed splurging on whatever I wanted.

Instead, I chose to put that money into an Opportunity Zone Fund, which I mentioned in the chapter on real estate. At a pre-determined time, your capital gains tax is due, but you get a 10% step up in the basis—meaning, if you invested $100,000, your basis is now $90,000. In addition, many of these Opportunity Zone funds take steps to lessen the need for coming out of pocket, by structuring dividends that would be otherwise be taxed as a repayment of principal. Finally, if you keep your money in the fund for a minimum of 10 years, the growth is treated like Roth money—the growth and gains are tax free on the federal level, even if there may be some state taxes. That's a big kicker for private individuals.

Note that, in January 2027, the Opportunity Zone 2.0 program will kick in, with an updated set of rules. As with all things that sound almost too good to be true, Opportunity Zones may not exist forever—but then again, there may be something different that could serve as another option. Talk to your CPA or financial advisor to learn more about what's available at the time you're reading this.

Note that this strategy can work with any type of capital gain. If you sell an office building, you can always roll it into another building with a 1031 exchange. Alternatively, if you sell and have a capital gain, you could pay the taxes—or put those dollars into an Opportunity Zone Fund.

SOLO 401(K)

Whether in traditional or Roth form, this is a secret financial weapon for any projects you do on the side as an independent contractor even if you have a retirement plan through your employer—although you also need to make sure everything is within your annual limits across plans. If you contribute to a traditional Solo 401(k), you benefit from the pre-tax deduction; with the Roth version, you're paying in with post-tax dollars, but the gains and withdrawals are tax-free. Either way, you can set aside considerably more retirement money, since you can contribute your portion as an employee as well as a profit-sharing component as the employer.

SELF-DIRECTED IRAS

Self-directed IRAs can be a powerful vehicle for increasing your wealth, expanding your options far beyond the usual rotation of stocks, bonds, and mutual funds. They are complicated, however, and many are best executed with the advice of a financial planner or CPA. For example, within a self-directed IRA you can own a commercial building where you're renting out space to a variety of businesses. You cannot, however, do so if your practice is located in one of the suites, if you are a part owner of any of the entities, or if your involvement is part of their success or failure. (That would be considered self-dealing.) That doesn't mean you're not involved in managing the property itself, because you own it. Ideally, you have rent checks coming into the self-directed IRA (i.e., not to you directly) as well as an asset that grows in value.

Coordination of Your Financial Care

Think of handling your finances as comparable to coordination of care. A patient comes to the hospital with a hip fracture, but they also have heart disease and diabetes. The primary care physician is coordinating, overseeing the global care. You have an endocrinologist, because the patient is diabetic, and their kidneys have an issue, so you've got a nephrologist. The cardiologist is there to monitor heart issues, and last but not least, the orthopedic surgeon is consulted because of the hip fracture that landed the patient there in the first place. It behooves the members of the team to coordinate care together, but realistically, nobody has the time to speak to one another. Everyone's relying on reading the chart notes.

That's the way you should think about your CPA, financial advisor, and attorney. They each need to know what the other is doing—because anything you do is likely to impact another part of your financial and legal health.

SHOULD I PAY OFF MY STUDENT LOANS?

There's no right or wrong answer. You've got to do the math. Unfortunately, I'm one of the many physicians who was under the mistaken impression from med school that I'd be able to deduct the interest—only to find out that it's not deductible over a certain income amount, and that figure is lower than you think. Depending on the interest rate environment, it can make sense to consolidate your loans at a lower rate. But, depending again on the rate, do you think you can earn more in the market or other investments while paying the loan minimum? I have colleagues from med school who were really anti-debt and focused on paying their loans down regardless of the rate. I preferred to see if I could do better with my investments. To each their own, right?

Another item to put into the calculation before you pay off any loans or consolidate with your spouse's loans: How would doing so impact your spouse? Speaking only of my personal experience, all of my loans were in my name alone, for a strategic if somewhat morbid reason. If I died, my spouse would not be on the hook for paying my loans back. Talk with your financial advisor about what makes sense in your situation.

Dad's Wisdom: Living Below Your Means

When I finished my training, my dad—an electrical engineer, and one of the hardest workers I've ever known—gave me a piece of advice that served me well. "The jump in salary you're going to get from finishing your fellowship to starting practice is probably going to be the biggest percentage increase you've ever seen in your life from an earning perspective," he said. "So, assess how you're living right now. Are you struggling to put food on the table? No, you're not. Are you able to pay your rent? Yes, you are. See if you can live for a year or two like you are now. Go out to a fancy dinner once in a while. See what it does for your lifestyle. See what it does for the dollars in your account and think about the growth you'll start seeing."

He was right, as parents so often are. Nothing can replace living below your means, and your outcomes will be impacted by a variety of outside factors such as what state you live in and your life stage, not to mention the overall state of the economy. (If you really want to push the limits on extreme frugality and savings strategies, take some time to research the FIRE (Financial Independence, Retire Early) movement.) Being wise with your money puts you in a more secure position, so that you don't have to make desperate decisions—and can take advantage of opportunities. It will get you through peaks and valleys in your career. And above all, it will give you the freedom to choose where you work, with whom you work, and how long you work . . . on your own terms.

YOUR LEGACY: TRUSTS & FOUNDATIONS

You've spent your life planning to be a physician, but when it comes to your legacy, there are two instruments to consider discussing with your financial and legal advisors.

- **Trusts.** If something happens to you, you don't want your heirs dealing with probate court and all the other headaches. Even when you're starting out and don't have that many assets, these are relatively easy and inexpensive to set up; and if it's done right, it will be simple to tell your attorney to add this property or that account without having to rewrite the entire document.

- **Charitable foundations.** As a 501(c)(3) organization, a private foundation is a nonprofit typically controlled and funded by an individual or family. As the welfare of animals is our biggest passion, my wife and I started a foundation focused on animal welfare-related causes. Yes, it's also a tax deduction, but more importantly it leverages the money in a way that gives us better bang for the buck in a cause we care deeply about—including growing the funds via investments. Donor-advised funds are an increasingly popular route, thanks to streamlined recordkeeping and the ability to establish them for significantly less than a private foundation.

PRACTICE PEARLS
Read the Room

We've all been there: You're at a big fundraising event and some blowhard is giving you way more detail than you need about how they performed some procedure or surgery, or bragging about how many patients they see. Meanwhile, you're thinking it's time to get up and refresh your cocktail, or wondering if there's an anesthesiologist nearby who can knock you out.

A better approach is to talk about anything other than medicine. Talk about economics, an off-the-beaten path vacation you recently enjoyed, a screenplay you're writing, or a Picasso exhibit that knocked your socks off. Be memorable for who you are and what you know, rather than just what you do.

Managing Your Money

A Wealth Advisor's Perspective

By Justin W. Breece JD, CDFA®, CEPA®

IN THE FINANCIAL INDUSTRY, it's almost automatic that you walk into client meetings—whether physicians or otherwise—under the assumption that everyone's goal is retirement. But I fear we're doing a disservice. To me, it's more important (both for me as an advisor, and you as a client) to understand how you are wired. In keeping with one of Amit's major themes throughout this book, I would suggest a better approach to wealth planning is to prioritize optionality. What is the number we need to achieve to give you the most and best options, whether you retire or not?

Even with high-net worth individuals, there's a tendency to look at things in a vacuum: Your money is going to do this, this, and this, and here are some financial products and advice that will achieve that. When working with clients, I believe the process should always lead with the "Why?" Why are we doing this in the first place? That reframes our thinking:

My money is doing X because I am trying to accomplish Y, which will allow me to do Z.

That facilitates an entirely different mindset. If your aim is retirement, we can work towards that. Alternatively, if you don't retire but know that you could, you can approach your job and mission every day with a heightened level of confidence and performance. You can think more clearly, and psychologically it gets you away from the fight-or-flight instinct. Hopefully you're doing the right thing to begin with, but it ensures you won't bend your ethics to recommend a gray-area procedure or treatment a patient doesn't need, just because the mortgage is due. It's a route to clarity, fulfillment, and freedom.

Barriers to Success

That said, you also need to understand how you can help us as financial advisors to do a better job of helping you navigate that route. I've worked with quite a few medical professionals over the years. Within the finance industry, I'll be frank, doctors have a reputation as clients. On the good side: Highly intelligent with a strong work discipline and focus. But there are some elements that make physicians challenging. If you can avoid the following traits, you're not only going to have a better relationship with your financial advisor, they're going to get better results for you. (I'm speaking in generalities, so these aren't meant to be taken personally—but be on the lookout for them creeping into your mindset.)

- **Herd mentality.** Physicians aren't alone in this; it's also common among professional athletes. When friends or colleagues jump in on a certain type of investment, everyone floods in at once without doing their due diligence. Spoiler alert: Investment stampedes never end well.

- **Lack of self-awareness.** One of our biggest mistakes as humans is that we tend to overestimate our skills. When we win, we attribute it to our brilliance, and when we lose, it's due to bad luck. That's just how we're wired. Unfortunately, that kind of overconfidence in your intelligence is amplified in doctors and can lead you to unwittingly take on more risk than you realize.

- **Second guessing.** By nature, many physicians are hands on. They want to know what's going on and have strong opinions about what should be done. Think of it this way, though: Every time there's a little bit of turbulence on a flight, would you go up to the cockpit, knock on the door, and tell the pilot what you think he should do? No, you wouldn't, and not just because the federal air marshal would take issue with you marching up the aisle. It's better to think of your financial advisor as the captain: They know far more about what it takes to land safely than you do.

- **Illiquidity.** Amit discussed real estate in chapter 8, and there's nothing wrong with having some real estate in your portfolio. But as he noted, it's essential to recognize that real estate is illiquid and it's easy to get overextended. I know some physicians who owned 10 or 20 rental homes during the Great Recession and lost everything.

- **Speculation.** No one sends me more emails than physicians asking "Hey, have you heard of this?", usually with some penny stock for an obscure biotech company or a cancer cure promoted by some genius doctor. Not long ago, I got called by a big-time cardiologist who wanted to know what I thought about meme coins, since he knew a colleague who'd raked in $25 million almost overnight. Speculation errors stem from a few different sources, usually overconfidence plus herd mentality. I'm not going to offer specific investing advice here, but remember the blinders that Amit referenced earlier in the book? If you're tempted by penny stocks, meme coins, or any other get-rich-quick schemes, you're better off keeping those blinders on.

Positive financial progress is often imperceptible and very slow. Bad things, however, tend to happen fast. As a result of some or all of those mistakes, I've seen way too many physicians who experience a material drop in wealth and blow up their entire financial balance sheet trying to get it all back. The pain is amplified, because it's embarrassing. They need to maintain the optics of a certain lifestyle, which leads to further bad decisions on how they're managing their practice, their families, and their personal health. It's insidious. Worse yet, their damaged ego makes them reticent to ask for help from a financial advisor or attorney, because that would mean admitting a mistake—and they'd rather wallow in misery.

A Quick Perspective on Debt

The majority of newer physicians walk through the door of their first practice with significant amounts of debt, especially and obviously student loans. I can't express strongly enough how important it is to have a partner to help you think through debt. Everyone approaches debt differently, and I've noticed there's major emotional hang-up in how people view it.

If you're confused, I totally get it. There's so much divergent advice on whether debt should be considered the worst thing in the world or nothing to worry about. One of the things I try to help clients understand, especially young medical professionals, is that there are times when debt is a good thing. Not all debt is bad; in fact, debt can be your friend in certain circumstances, but it needs to be in the context of the overall plan. There are times, in fact, when debt becomes an asset.

It all comes back to your Why and what you're trying to accomplish. Is there a reason you have a hang-up about debt? Or conversely, why do you have so much debt, and why are you continuing to let it be an albatross around your neck? A good advisor will help get your priorities straight, sequence how you should be approaching debt versus assets and savings, and develop a strategy.

These are extraordinary times, and we've seen some pretty crazy swings on interest rates. There are times when you want to turn up the dial and tackle some of that debt, and other times where that's the last thing you should be doing—in fact, you're better off adding debt to get the additional operating leverage of almost-free money. When you get locked rates at a low level, there's a high likelihood your investments are going to perform better, even in a basic money market, when you include the tax benefits.

Optionality and Passive Income

Debt also needs to be juxtaposed against the power of compounding interest, which truly is one of the few gifts in life and the closest thing in this world to a free lunch. Albert Einstein called it the eighth wonder of the world for a very good reason. I'm a guest speaker in Finance at Arizona State University once a semester, and even at that level, I always start with the basics of compounding interest. There's no better way to put the odds in your favor.

On social media, passive income has developed a reputation as the Holy Grail. And sure, who doesn't want cash coming in without extra work attached? Unfortunately, there tends to be a gravitational pull towards illiquid assets (such as homes) as the route to financial freedom. I constantly hear, especially among medical professionals, sentiments such as "My goal is to have 10 homes and rent them out, I'm going to get a check every month, and then I'm set." But if they did the math, it wouldn't necessarily pencil out in return on investment. Moreover, in many cases, there's nothing passive about real estate. Real estate is often painfully active, tax-inefficient income. Middle-of-the-night calls to the plumber, if you can even find one. Property taxes. HOAs. Renters who trash the place or don't want to pay their bills.

Yes, passive income is a way to achieve optionality, but what are the asset classes that give you the best chance of taking advantage of compounding interest? You can structure corporate bonds. You can structure treasuries. These are just two examples of instruments—among many—that you can know with near certitude the instant the interest is going to hit your account, with precision down to the penny. That's passive. That's powerful. That's liberating.

I don't say that to demean any other passive income strategy, because there's a time and a place for everything, including real estate. But liquidity and possible downside risks need to be part of your equation, balanced against the probability of success. Beyond the math, remember that optionality is also a quality-of-life issue. Ideally, passive income should decrease your stress, not add to it. There's an opportunity cost to the phone calls, paperwork, and meetings required to manage a property. Maybe you'd rather be doing something else with your time, while enjoying one of the no-hassle, super-tax-efficient income streams that you could deploy instead.

Tips on Selecting a Wealth Advisor

Choosing a wealth advisor is one of the most consequential decisions you will make in your career. One of our most important purposes is to serve as an emotional filter: keeping people from making unforced errors under stress. If I were interviewing a wealth advisor, I would want to know:

- What's their constitutional makeup?

- Where are they in life?

- Are they anchored, and if so, what are they anchored to?

- Above all, when emotions are running high, how is this person built?

Many of the financial products on the market are commoditized. Even so, certain people will deploy them better than others. Put a 16-year-old in one Lamborghini and put Michael Schumacher in another, and you're going to get different results.

Looking at the situation from a more holistic standpoint: What's the driver like? Does this person get me? What are their motivations and goals? Do they understand and align with my ultimate goals? Building out and implementing the solutions still takes a tremendous amount of expertise, but understanding your financial advisor's own "Why" is just as important as yours. Because if you don't feel like they care about you at the deepest level, or that they are executing the plan truly in your best interest, it's not going to work. It's too mentally taxing, too emotional, and there's too much at stake.

Anyone can tell you to put your 401(k) into 65% stocks and 35% bonds, or whatever is appropriate for your age. That's table stakes. As a physician, however, your life is more complicated, whether you like it or not: You're in a high-income space with lots of regulations, so it's not just about growing your stock portfolio. You need to think about it from a multi-disciplinary standpoint. A lot of people on the wealth advisory side might be rockstars at growing assets, but at the end of the day, if you're not doing it on a tax-efficient basis, you're hindering the ultimate result.

A skilled financial advisor goes beyond serving as a trusted resource with your money. Once again, that's table stakes. They need to bring a level of imagination to the process that extends far beyond your portfolio balance. To me, that should include helping you dream a little bit more, to see yourself and your life in a different way that maybe others haven't.

As a wealth advisor, I ask a lot of questions, helping people lead themselves to sound decisions that will lead to certain outcomes. I'm not able to play Socrates and ask you questions directly here, so I encourage you and a financial advisor to engage in that dialogue, starting now. On the face of it, wealth planning is about money, but that's secondary to your quality of life, who you are as a person, and what avenues can bring you maximum fulfilment.

Justin W. Breece JD, CDFA®, CEPA® *is a comprehensive plan-ning-based wealth advisor and portfolio manager director with more than 20 years of experience in financial services. He is the owner and managing director of Breece Private Wealth Management in Scottsdale, Arizona.*

Investment products and services are offered through Wells Fargo Advisors Financial Network, LLC (WFAFN), Member SIPC. Breece Private Wealth Management of TSG Wealth Management is a separate entity from WFAFN.

PRACTICE PEARLS
Play Like A Peer

In residency, we'd often see the results of a procedure done "less than perfectly," such as a fracture fixed with inadequate hardware or non-anatomic reduction. During the morning trauma conference, we residents naturally would comment on or question the skill of the surgeon who'd done the work. Our ortho trauma chief called these cases a *horrendioma*, which didn't appear in your medical terminology textbook but you can guess its meaning. But beyond the dark humor, he would quickly also tell us never to badmouth or overtly criticize the work done by another doctor. He'd say, "They did their best. Perhaps they don't have the luxury of having a team of residents and fellows to help them. Perhaps they did the surgery on their own, in the middle of the night."

Understand the rules of engagement.

—DR. AMIT SAHASRABUDHE

Managing Your Money

A Retired CPA's Perspective

By Rachel Cooper CPA (Retired)

AS A RETIRED CPA whose practice specialized in taxes, my function was similar to being a doctor, trying to diagnose symptoms and prescribe solutions to keep your financial standing healthy. Some of my clients were employee physicians, and they were very happy that way—they have no desire to go out on their own. Others navigated private practice and stayed committed to that path. Still others were absorbed by private equity, and needed to answer the pressing question, "How do we exit the business gracefully and take care of our employees?"

Each path is different, and each physician has their own take on what they believe is most important—which is why a conversation with your CPA starts with your goals. Are you looking purely for the most tax savings? Putting away as much money as possible for retirement? Looking to make as much money as possible right now and you can worry about retirement later? Or, are you open to the idea of making things a bit more administratively complex and time consuming in order to save some tax while achieving bigger goals?

In the world of taxes, there's always give and take in play.

While I realize you want to keep up with the latest news in *The Wall Street Journal*, that information isn't always correct or applicable to your individual circumstances. There's a lot of interpretation involved at the intersection of accounting and federal, state, and local laws. Even though CPAs deal in numbers, staying on top of the words in our ever-changing tax laws is a critical piece of the puzzle. Depending on what state or states you reside or practice in, there's a dizzying array of tax credits, rules, and regulations that need to be incorporated into the mix, whether you are W-2 or out on your own.

Tips for Employee Physicians

If you're an employee physician, everything starts with making sure that you have enough withholding on your W-2. I've had many doctors tell me, "This is what the payroll table said was correct for my withholding." The problem is, when you're making $200,000–$300,000, the payroll tables don't account for that, plus you need to incorporate the other taxable events that are going on aside from your job, such as investment or rental property income. Are you receiving grant money? Depending on how the grant is structured and where you live, you may need to pay tax on it. Although the taxes are not withheld on your W-2, the government wants its cut.

In many cases, that could mean withholding an extra few hundred or thousand dollars each paycheck, depending on a variety of factors. Rather than guessing, the most accurate way to determine the right figure is to talk with your CPA and do some tax planning. With your W-2, net pay stub, and a list of your other sources of income (including investments, rental properties, etc.), they can help ensure your withholding is appropriate and that you don't get hit with a big tax bill and underpayment penalties. Doing the calculations upfront can save you a lot of headaches on the back end.

It's also important to recognize that your situation will vary year-to-year and sometimes during the year. You don't need to talk to your CPA every month, but you should check in at least annually or anytime there's a major life change. In such cases, it doesn't hurt to reach out, provide an update, and ask "How am I doing? What do I need to tweak?"

Tips for Private Practice

One of the first hurdles for someone who's starting out in private practice is all the setup fees, legal fees, and other expenses associated with going out on your own. In our office, you'll often hear us cite the time-tested advice to not be **"penny wise and pound foolish."** In an era in which everyone seemingly wants to sue everybody for the smallest little thing, you've got to go through the steps to protect yourself from the outset. That's the best way to capitalize on the potential wealth of being in private practice, while mitigating your risks.

Beyond a professional accountant, a good bookkeeper is paramount when you're running a private practice. Too many doctors think that it'll be sufficient to track everything on spreadsheets. Here's the reality: You already have a ton of responsibilities, and the last thing you need is to be swamped in the minutia how much money is coming in and going out. Yes, you need to understand that from a 10,000-foot level, but leave the details to experts who can watch what's going on and double check everything.

Other key players to include in the process are a business attorney (with medical law experience), who can help you navigate the liability insurance and different entity types that are best for reaching your goals, and a financial advisor who handles your portfolio and understands the tradeoffs between maximizing retirement funds and paying the least amount of tax.

The best client relationships I had were when I can talk with the business attorney and financial advisor without the client present—allowing all three of us to get on the same page before presenting you, the client, with a plan of action. The financial advisor knows the investment goals and the attorney knows the risk situation. My mission is to bring everything to minimize the tax on both sides, given the current, expiring, and anticipated tax laws, and when it's best to have a taxable event.

Regardless of your structure, having a separate entity that tracks your practice income and expenses means separating everything, including a separate bank account and credit card. If you put everything through your personal accounts, you're opening yourself up to a lawsuit: The moment you commingle business and personal funds, you've done what's known as *piercing the corporate veil*—which means that expensive malpractice insurance you purchased may not be able to protect your personal assets. It's worth spending the minor amount in extra bank fees to avoid unintended consequences.

What type of legal entity is best for your practice, whether a Professional Corporation (MD PC or DO PC) or Professional Limited Liability Company (PLLC), is a discussion you need to have with your CPA and medical business attorney. The pros, cons, and regulations of each vary significantly enough from state to state that it's beyond the scope of this book.

I do want to comment, however, on what's known as an S-Corp, which is a tax treatment elected through the IRS, not a state-level entity type. Therefore, it has implications for how you run your business, your ownership structure, whether you're on payroll, and a lot of other administrative aspects.

S-Corps are great for one-person owners and one shareholder, and they're very popular with physicians because they are tax effective. But they are also very rigid, with lots of stringent rules and regulations, and it's easy to make bad decisions if you're not careful. I'll give you two real-life examples.

Dr. Jones was doing great in his practice and wanted to buy a building with some of the profits. Unbeknownst to me, he used his S Corp for the transaction. Almost a year after he did the deal, right before the end of the year, we had our annual call. I asked him how things were going. "Oh, we bought a building," he said. "I'll send you the information." When I received the paperwork and saw that the property had been bought in the name of the S Corp, it gave me an instant migraine. Because the property had increased in value, he couldn't get it out of the business without paying the capital gains immediately—it was effectively stuck in the S Corp. The lesson is that too many physicians reflexively think "Oh, it's all under my practice, I'll just put it in one thing"—but the most tax efficient way of executing such a transaction is to buy the building in a separate LLC and have your practice rent it from the LLC.

The other related eventuality to keep in mind is that you someday might want to add another doctor as a partner, which should always be done using a separate LLC, not your S Corp. Here's one of the common mistakes I've seen: A doctor has a PC that's formed as an S Corp, and the partner buys in at 25% and the original owner retains 75%. At some point, the majority owner wants to take distributions out—but the rules of an S Corp require that those occur at a pro rata percentage. In other words, if he or she takes out $750,000, the partner needs to receive $250,000, whether or not they have earned or produced the work or the revenue for that.

When you get into situations with multiple partners, you may want to have an LLC that handles everything, and each doctor has their own S Corp that goes up to the LLC above. (There are also some interactions with various Medicare laws, so an attorney who is well versed in medical laws is essential to ensure this structure doesn't cause unintended issues.)

Planning for the Future

One recommendation that you might not hear elsewhere is to find a CPA who is young—similar in age to you or a few years older. When you do that, you can both grow in your careers together, without having to change horses midstream. Continuity helps more than you might realize. One of my doctor clients has been with my practice for 20 years, and the entire family relies on me for all sorts of questions, whether the wife is calling me about a transaction from three years ago or one of the kids has a question about their own finances. I've become a trusted advisor who knows the inner workings of how the family works, in addition to how the practice, real estate, and all of their entities all come together. Nine times out of 10, they'll call me before they call their attorney.

Once you get along in your career and you've started to build some wealth, there are many opportunities to create trusts and foundations. They could be causes that are near and dear to your heart that you want to support in the future, or ways of supporting your children or other loved ones through college and beyond. There are myriad strategies that can be useful at various life stages, and your CPA can be a helpful advisor every step of the way.

The biggest mistake I see among physicians—although it's not limited to them—is not asking for help. If you believe you know more than you do, it's easy to find yourself far down a bumpy road where it's difficult to recover, triggering tax penalties, IRS audits, and other unpleasant unintended consequences.

The sooner you can enlist the help of advisors, the better off you'll be. Yes, I know it's expensive. Yes, I know the value isn't obvious at the beginning. But having good, reliable, and ethical people will get you moving in the right direction for the long run.

My final thought is that you're paying your CPA for advice, so it's probably wise to take it. . . even though you may not like it or it may cost a little bit to do what they're suggesting. At the same time, I always tell my clients, "If you don't like what I'm saying and you believe that there's another way, please, by all means, find someone that can explain it to me a different way." As CPAs, we're always open to looking at new information—just as you are when you're treating patients. We know what we know, but you can't possibly know the details of thousands of pages of constantly changing tax law, unless you've somehow stumbled upon an accountant with a photographic memory and recall.

Rachel Cooper *is a retired CPA, and former partner of Pescatore Cooper PLC in Phoenix has more than 25 years' experience in individual and small business income tax compliance. She* *specializes in individual and small to medium-sized business taxation including consulting and planning, as well as payroll and sales tax reporting and compliance.*

Disclaimer: Tax laws are constantly changing and increasing in complexity. The information provided is for informational or educational purposes only and does not constitute personalized, professional financial advice.

A penny wise and pound foolish.

—ROBERT BURTON, 17TH-CENTURY
ENGLISH SCHOLAR

CHAPTER 10
Wax On, Wax Off

Ikigai and Finding Meaning
through Optionality

IT'S A CLICHÉ THAT DOCTORS are supposed to retire to playing golf every day or cruising around on their yacht named *Knot on Call* or *Recovery Room*. I attempted to address the first option during the spring semester of my junior year in college, when I had to take an elective for gym credits. "I'm going to be a physician," I thought. "I need to know how to play golf."

On the first day of class at the indoor driving range, the instructor comes up behind me, doesn't say hi, doesn't introduce himself, and the first words out of his mouth are: "Oh, you're never going to have a good golf swing."

And I just turned around and looked at him. "Thanks. Might I ask why?"

I'm athletic and had been a decent baseball player as a kid, so his comment was perplexing to me. He went into a goofy explanation of how the ratio of my shoulder width to my arm length prevented me from taking the club back properly.

I looked at him again, and said, "So why am I taking this class then?"

I finished the class, didn't enjoy it, and now I'm one of those oddball doctors who doesn't chase a little white ball around on weekends. I don't have many regrets in life, but the non-golf gym option was to learn how to sail in Key West.

What Keeps You in the Game?

When I started practicing medicine, for some reason that I couldn't articulate, I always had a notion that I wanted to retire by 50. Why 50? I don't know, it seemed like a nice even number. Even at the age of 26, when I finished residency and fellowship, I romanticized the idea that it would give me extra time living a life I wanted. What I told myself back then is that I would bust my butt as much as I could, and hopefully avoid foolish decisions like living beyond my means.

I envisioned three possible scenarios:

1. If I was financially able to retire and no longer wanted to practice medicine when I hit 50, then I would step away.

2. If I wanted to keep practicing, I'd keep going.

3. If I wasn't financially able to stop working, I wouldn't be mad at myself, as long as I'd tried my best and hadn't done anything dumb.

As the half-century mark got closer, my original reasoning held up. I was able to articulate my reasons and pulled the trigger two years early. Instead of postponing, I preponed.

When word got around, though, my colleagues had questions. Why? What are you doing? What are you going to do? And I kept thinking to myself, "Well, I don't understand why you're still doing this. You're 60 and still full steam ahead, seeing 40 patients a day? You're 65 and still doing surgery? Are you sure your spouse is on board with this?"

It wasn't necessarily a criticism of what they were doing,

but more a matter of trying to understand their reason for why—assuming they weren't staying in the game purely for the money.

A few months later, I found a book that offered a partial explanation: *Ikigai: The Japanese Secret to a Long and Happy Life*. Conceptually, *ikigai* can be defined as what gives an individual meaning or purpose in their life. As I read, it dawned on me that I'd had my own blinders on. I felt like I'd been given a lesson from Mr. Miyagi in *The Karate Kid*, or the modern-day version of his wisdom in *Cobra Kai*. Wax on, wax off: A repetitive motion that only reveals its importance later.

If someone hops out of bed in the morning with a burning desire to practice neurology at the age of 68, and they're still performing at a high level, who am I to say "There's so much more to life. Why are you still doing this?" As long as they're actively making the choice, that's their prerogative.

But that isn't everyone. I hear some colleagues claim they don't know what else that they would do. For those who've set themselves up financially, partial retirement or programs like Doctors Without Borders can scratch that itch without being tethered to the office every day. Others assert that they still love practicing medicine full time, while looking downright miserable and treating patients as if it's a burden. For a lot of them, I question whether it truly is their ikigai. They may not have found it, or maybe it changed from the original single-minded pursuit of becoming a physician.

Too many of us put our blinders on and the roadmap looks like this: "Well, if I want to get there, I've got to do A, B, C, D, and E, in that order, and nothing else." Somewhere along the way, though, we lose sight of why we were truly doing that. We feel caught in the situation, wanting to believe that's what gives us life's meaning or purpose. For a lot of physicians, if you asked them to be honest with themselves, I suspect they might say, "Yeah, I'd rather do something else" but they find themselves unable to make a lateral move or add on or do something different.

If you're in your 20s when you're reading this book, you're going to have a different perspective from someone who's in their 40s or 50s, but the principles remain the same. There's no guaranteeing that what's new and exciting to you now will still be that way as your career progresses.

Think back to when you were applying to med schools and an admissions officer asked you why you wanted to be a doctor. You would have been foolish to respond, "Because I want to earn $300,000 a year." If you had, I suspect your application would have ended up in the slush pile. Even if money had been one of your top three factors at the time, it couldn't be the only reason to go through years of pain and hard work, so you were smart enough to answer with some version of "Well, I want to help people."

When I chose to retire early from the clinical practice of medicine, one of the main reasons was that it was no longer my ikigai, even though helping patients was still as rewarding as it was on the first day I stitched up a patient with a torn ACL. You may still find yourself with that burning passion you had on day one, and that's great. But if you find yourself having a shift in mindset over the years, what I hope to convey in this book is that you have myriad options—thanks to your highly marketable medical degree—to navigate through or around the challenges.

Your Annual Ikigai Checkup

So, how do you monitor those sometimes-subtle mental shifts and readjust your roadmap? In the corporate world, they have you do annual reviews with your staff or employees. I'm a proponent of that, even though they're a pain in the butt, and when I ran my small practice, I did them with my staff.

More important, though, was that I did my own personal review every year.

- What was this past year like?

- What was successful, and what wasn't?

- With the gift of 20/20 hindsight, what should I have done differently?

- What am I going to differently going forward?

This exercise in self-reflection needed to be about more than just the money, that I made X thousands of dollars more or less. My intention was to reflect on how I'd grown, what I'd learned, and what other options I wanted to explore. I had an intuitive sense of ikigai before I even knew the word.

There's a difference between being happy with something and being content with what you have. You may have heard of the hedonic treadmill, where you set a goal and start running, yet once you get there it's not enough. In an everyday application, think about an entry-level worker making $15 an hour and they get bumped to $16. That's great, helps a little bit with paying the bills, maybe a date night. But within a few weeks, they start thinking it would be even nicer to get to $17.50, so they start running faster. They're constantly in the pursuit of happiness, but never get there—because they're never content with what they have.

That's magnified for physicians, because the numbers

are so much larger. For a lot of us, the treadmill turns into lifestyle escalation: "I made a record amount last year, but now I have to earn $X-plus because I've made choices a little beyond my means."

As you're going through life, nobody can tell you what your roadmap is, let alone your ikigai. If you're waiting for the universe to tell you, while you're just chugging away on the treadmill, remember that not making a choice is also a choice.

Nor is this just about you. Your decisions, and the timing of them, impact your significant other and family. If your spouse is still working a 9-to-5, what does that mean for your overall plans? You might be OK going fishing or playing golf every day, but it throws a wrench into traveling the world or moving to Ecuador. Likewise, if your spouse retires and you're still on call, how's that going to work? There's no simple answer, and I'm not saying I have one. But expectations are important, and it's a conversation you need to have.

This book has covered a lot of topics that can provide optionality if you choose to pursue them. Understand that they're not the end-all-be-all. If you still derive meaning, purpose, and joy from what you're doing on a day-to-day basis—whether that's seeing patients or consulting for pharma—then keep doing it.

Ultimately, it's up to you to define your medical career roadmap for yourself, up to and including retirement, whatever form it takes. I believe there's no better way to prepare yourself for the future than giving yourself optionality and the opportunity to pivot. The more avenues you have available to yourself, the clearer your mind can be about making those decisions when the time comes.

So, start building your roadmap now; it's never too early, or too late. And perhaps it starts with exploring your why: What's your Ikigai?

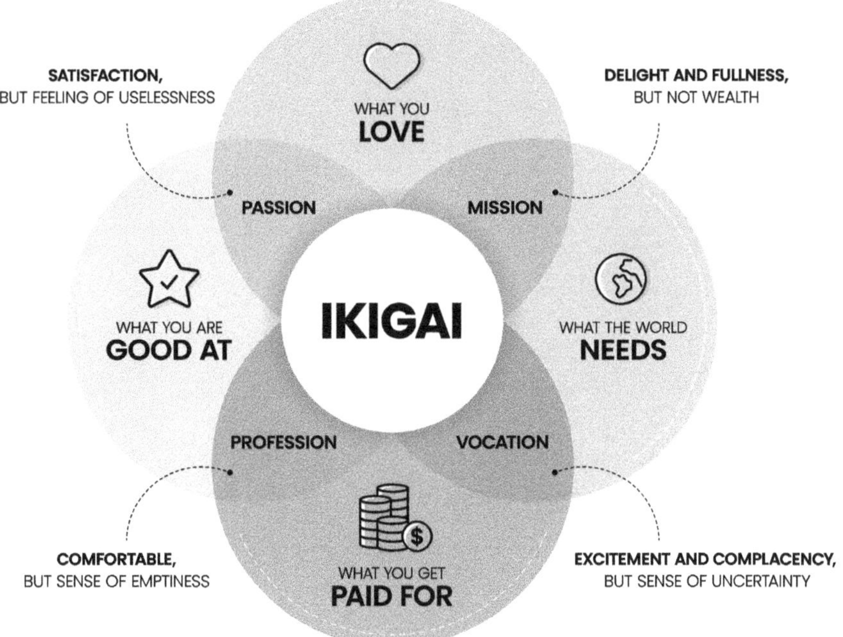

Afterword

A LOT OF ASPIRING PHYSICIANS walk into medical school on day 1 with an altruistic mentality. You want to help people, and that's a great foundation. But what's equally true: If you're not taking care of yourself and your family with a financial plan and long-term perspective, it will eventually come back to bite you.

I was one of those rogue physicians that started my own practice right out of residency, with a vision of doing everything from sports and family medicine to wellness and nutrition to covering high school sports. While it was arguably a risky move at the time, I'm still running that practice more than 20 years later.

A few years after I began practicing, I joined a sports medicine group—and within three months, I recognized that the business wasn't running the way it should. I looked at the books, talked with the business manager and the other four physicians, and said, "Hey, I think we're missing out on a lot. Would you be interested in having me be the managing partner of the group?" The answer was an overwhelming yes. Soon after that, it was off to the races. We hired another doctor, I renegotiated the leases and all of our vendor contracts, I found a new accountant to put together a building fund, and eventually we expanded our practice with multiple high school and professional teams.

While that was my first venture, I was always interested in business, even though I don't have any formal training in it. When people ask me "How do you start a business?" or "How do you grow a business?", the answer comes down to math, hustle, and surrounding yourself with the right people. The foundation is smart, solid business partners, and then you supplement that with a savvy team of accountants and financial planners who you can bounce ideas off and will help manage the professional side of your career.

I first met Amit at that point in my career, and we were business partners for a long period of time. We created and implemented multiple businesses within medicine, and he was a classic example of the power of surrounding yourself with the right people. Equally important, we had the same values in both business and in medicine. That allowed us to accomplish a lot, and it also helped us get through some significant and complex challenges. We could sit down in a room, talk through the issues, and between us we'd figure out an action plan to make things happen. Plus, we also had a lot of fun along the way to building our portfolio of profitable ventures.

This book is a fantastic playbook to increase your own potential for using a medical career as a route to financial success; I know it works, because I experienced elements of it firsthand. I'll also tell you this: You can educate yourself on the math and assemble a great team, but what this book can't do is give you the hustle to make it happen. You need to have a plan, and it needs to be applied with a lot of dedication, time, and effort in order to accomplish your goals, whatever they may be. And, I should add, you can't force it and try to do everything all at once.

For all the exponential advances in medicine—from

medical treatments to robotics and AI—the amount of exposure to business most doctors receive during schooling and training remains minimal, if it exists at all. For too many of us, the expectation is that you show up and magic happens. Once you're in the real world, though, you need to have an interest in business to get better at it.

As an employee, that can mean anything from taking on side hustles to being smart about savings and retirement. Starting a private practice, joining a group, or building a business entity is a completely different animal. You need to have entrepreneurial spirit and tough skin, because there are contracts to negotiate, staff to hire and manage, and business partners to work with—including navigating the occasional conflict or unforeseen disaster. It quickly expands beyond the reasons you went into medicine.

Your plan and perspective include, of course, what you want the path to look like as you get deeper into your career. I'm a good example of what Amit described as the type of physician for whom retirement wasn't my priority or my ikigai. I love what I do. Even upon reaching a point where my financial situation would enable me to never work again, I simply enjoy sports medicine. The format may change, but I expect to work in some capacity for as long as I can—just with less volume and more focus on the stuff that I think is fun.

Looking back over the past 25 years, I've seen the practice side get tougher. Reimbursement from the insurance companies has gone down, so it seems like every year you work harder to make the same or even a little less money. They control all the forms you need to fill out, the denials, and (in many cases) how much money you can make. That positive altruistic feeling of being a physician can get wasted when you're just treading water with your financial expectations and outcomes.

I don't say that, however, to sound defeatist. Among the key takeaways from this book is that you absolutely can take better control of your fate, especially the freedom to be more financially secure.

Bottom line, I would have loved to have had this book when I started out. Almost 100% of what I did early on was trial and error, with the occasional act of blind stupidity. When I talked to my residency director and some of the other docs in the community about my plans, I got a lot of side eyes and raised eyebrows. Rather than offering encouragement, more than a few said words to the effect of "You probably shouldn't do that."

I dove in headfirst anyway, to see what would happen, and I was fortunate to meet Amit along my path. Your roadmap will be different, whether you choose to run and grow a practice, start a side gig or passive income stream, or simply become more knowledgeable about the business of medicine, reimbursement, and how it all works. Apply enough hustle and you'll create a situation where you can cut back on the tasks you don't enjoy, pivot and do something completely different, or hang it up altogether to teach yoga or travel the world. In the end, it's about giving yourself options.

—Erik J. Dean, DO

Acknowledgments

I CAN'T BEGIN TO ACCOUNT for all the people in my life who have brought me to this point, but I'd like to thank a few of the people who directly or indirectly spurred on the idea of writing this book.

My maternal grandmother...who brainwashed me into becoming a physician.

My maternal grandfather...from whom I inherited business savvy and insight.

My paternal grandfather...from whom I inherited the skill and manual dexterity to fix things, which certainly helps as an orthopedic surgeon.

My mom...from whom I learned to care for others and the concept of paying it forward. One of the drivers in writing this book was my belief that these topics aren't taught to physicians. The field of medicine has been remarkable for me; so, the least I could do is get the next generation thinking about their roadmap.

My dad...from whom I learned that there is no substitute for hard work. Hearing his story from childhood in a village in India to having multiple patents credited to his name—and all the hard work in between that it took to get there—instilled that same drive in me.

My wife Amrita...who supported me when I almost resigned from residency, saying, "If you're not happy, it isn't worth it. We will figure it out." She was also the first person to ever tell me that I was more than a doctor, that being a physician isn't the only thing that identifies you, even if I wasn't ready to believe that at the time.

My brother Adit. . . who I've always said is the smarter of the brothers and who I can always count on to challenge my perspective on matters. And engraved in my mind is the memory of how hard my brother shed tears of joy when Dr. Freddie Fu called me to offer a spot in the Pitt ortho residency program, a few months after I hadn't matched.

My sister-in-law Ujjaini. . . with whom I share more than one personality trait. And who—in addition to being unfailingly supportive—is such a voracious reader that if she likes this book, I know it's a good book.

My cousin Parul. . . who was the only one that didn't say something along the lines of "It'll be OK and it'll work out" when I didn't match. Instead, she told me exactly what I felt and actually wanted to hear: "You got screwed."

My cousin Suneel. . . my best friend growing up. And from whom we all can learn to always smile and be happy, no matter the circumstance. I have always admired that.

Justin Breece. . . both my financial advisor and close friend. Together we've shared many laughs with respect to old '80s movie quotes and created a very unique, diverse investment strategy/portfolio.

Rachel Cooper. . . both my CPA and close friend. In addition to being outstanding in her field, I appreciate that I can call or text her literally any time of day (including tax season!) with my latest harebrained idea and she answers.

Dr. Freddie Fu. . . the late, distinguished, and world-renowned Chairman of Orthopedics at University of Pittsburgh. Family was very important to him and he treated all his residents/fellows along with their spouses as family. I can never thank him enough for the 5:30 a.m. phone call offering me a spot in his residency program. Thank you, Dr. Fu, for taking a chance on me and giving me the opportunity.

Dr. Bruce Ziran... the ortho trauma attending who talked me off the ledge when I was at peak frustration and ready to quit during residency.

Dr. Gary Gruen... the ortho trauma attending who taught me about the benefit of securing multiple state licenses before you have baggage, and who taught me never to badmouth another physician.

Dr. James Lubowitz... my fellowship director in Taos, New Mexico, who was a whiz at the business side of medicine and taught me a ton of strategies that paid off over the course of my career. Notably, he was the one who advised me to attend a conference about business in orthopedics instead of a cartilage course back in 2007, which forever changed my trajectory. He planted the seed for my interest in the business and optionalities within medicine.

Dr. Doug Freedberg... who was the person I was angling to sit next to at dinner when I was looking for a new job, described in chapter 1. He shared his own experience about his first employer, and I vividly remember his words to me: "You know, it's amazing how many of us think we know what we're doing but have no clue. We don't get it right. Somebody ought to write a damn book about this." I've had that quote from him in my head ever since.

Dr. Erik Dean... my former business partner, with whom I implemented many of the strategies described in this book. Erik is an example of a physician who has leveraged his medical degree to go far beyond just taking care of patients. In fact, it was his brainchild for us partners to buy a building and rent out suites to referral sources.

About the Author

AMIT SAHASRABUDHE, MD, MS is a retired orthopedic surgeon, entrepreneur, investor, and CEO of an AI-driven health-tech startup. He practiced orthopedic surgery for nearly 17 years before retiring early—not only because he was financially able to, but because clinical medicine no longer provided the sense of purpose he was seeking.

Having navigated the realities of medical training, practice, and life beyond the exam room, Dr. Sahasrabudhe wrote *The Physician's Roadmap to Personal and Financial Freedom* to address the critical gaps never taught in medical school or residency. Through this book, he hopes to pay it forward by helping physicians design careers—and lives—defined by choice, flexibility, and fulfillment.

Help Other Readers Find this Book

If you found this book useful, I'd be grateful if you shared a brief review on the platform where you purchased it.

Reviews help readers decide which books to trust—and they help independent authors continue creating valuable work.

Thank you for being part of this book's journey.